If you have a home computer with
internet access you may:

• request an item to be placed on hold

• renew an item that is not overdue

• view titles and due dates checked out on your card

• view your own outstanding fines

To view your patron record from your home computer:
Click on the NSPL homepage: http://nspl.suffolk.lib.ny.us

North Shore Public Library

GREAT SPORTS TEAMS

THE NEW YORK KNICKS

JOHN F. GRABOWSKI

LUCENT
BOOKS®

THOMSON
————— ✦ —————™
GALE

San Diego • Detroit • New York • San Francisco • Cleveland
New Haven, Conn. • Waterville, Maine • London • Munich

Cover Photo: New York Knicks star Latrell Sprewell slam dunks the basketball.

© 2003 by Lucent Books. Lucent Books is an imprint of The Gale Group, Inc., a division of Thomson Learning, Inc.

Lucent Books® and Thomson Learning™ are trademarks used herein under license.

For more information, contact
Lucent Books
27500 Drake Rd.
Farmington Hills, MI 48331-3535
Or you can visit our Internet site at http://www.gale.com

LIBRARY OF CONGRESS CATALOGING-IN-PUBLICATION DATA

Grabowski, John F.
   The New York Knicks / by John F. Grabowski.
      p. cm. — (Great sports teams)
Summary: Discusses the history, formation, development, and popularity of the New York Knicks basketball team, including a look at individual players who have had an impact on the success of the team.
Includes bibliographical references (p.) and index.
   ISBN 1-56006-944-9
   1. New York Knickerbockers (Basketball team)—History—Juvenile literature. [1. New York Knickerbockers (Basketball team)—History. 2. Basketball—History] I. Title. II. Great sports teams (Lucent Books)
   GV885.52.N4 G73 2003
   796.323'64'097471—dc21

                                          2002151713

Printed in the United States of America

Contents

FOREWORD

Former Supreme Court chief justice Warren Burger once said he always read the sports section of the newspaper first because it was about humanity's successes, while the front page listed only humanity's failures. Millions of people across the country today would probably agree with Burger's preference for tales of human endurance, record-breaking performances, and feats of athletic prowess. Although these accomplishments are far beyond what most Americans can ever hope to achieve, average people, the fans, do want to affect what happens on the field of play. Thus, their role becomes one of encouragement. They cheer for their favorite players and team and boo the opposition.

ABC Sports president Roone Arledge once attempted to explain the relationship between fan and team. Sport, said Arledge, is "a set of created circumstances—artificial circumstances—set up to frustrate a man in pursuit of a goal. He has to have certain skills to overcome those obstacles—or even to challenge them. And people who don't have those skills cheer him and admire him." Over a period of time, the admirers may develop a rabid—even irrational—allegiance to a particular team. Indeed, the word "fan" itself is derived from the word "fanatic," someone possessed by an excessive and irrational zeal. Sometimes this devotion to a team is because of a favorite player; often it is because of where a person lives, and, occasionally, it is because of a family allegiance to a particular club.

Whatever the reason, the bond formed between team and fan often defies reason. It may be easy to understand the appeal of the New York Yankees, a team that has gone to the World Series an incredible thirty-eight times and won twenty-six championships, nearly three times as many as any other major league baseball team. It is more difficult, though, to comprehend the fanaticism of Chicago Cubs fans, who faithfully follow the progress of a team that hasn't won a World Series since 1908. Regardless, the Cubs have surpassed the 2 million mark in home attendance in fourteen of the last seventeen years. In fact, their two highest totals were posted in 1999 and 2000, when the team finished in last place.

Each volume in Lucent's Great Sports Teams series examines a team that has left its mark on the "American sports consciousness." Each book looks at the history and tradition of the club in an attempt to understand its appeal and the loyalty—even passion—of its fans. Each volume also examines the lives and careers of people who played significant roles in the team's history. Players, managers, coaches, and front-office executives are represented.

Endnoted quotations help bring the text in each book to life. In addition, all books include an annotated bibliography and a For Further Reading list to supply students with sources for conducting additional individual research.

No one volume can hope to explain fully the mystique of the New York Yankees, Boston Celtics, Dallas Cowboys, or Montreal Canadiens. The Lucent Great Sports Teams series, however, gives interested readers a solid start on the road to understanding the mysterious bond that exists between modern professional sports teams and their devoted followers.

The Basketball Capital of the World

To millions of people, New York is the basketball capital of the world. Kids throughout the city's five boroughs hone their skills in school yards, driveways, and anywhere else a hoop can be mounted. Many of them dream of following in the footsteps of Bob Cousy, Kareem Abdul-Jabbar, Connie Hawkins, and dozens of other natives of the Big Apple who graduated to NBA stardom. Most dream of playing for the city's basketball heroes, the New York Knickerbockers, popularly known as the Knicks.

The City Game

It is for good reason that Dr. James Naismith's 1891 invention of basketball became known as the City Game. It adapted well to urban areas since it did not require as large a playing surface as, for example, baseball or football. It could be played wherever a hoop could be hung on a wall or from a pole, as well as at playgrounds and gyms. Driveways eventually became a favorite site for one-on-one games between two competitors.

Another reason for the sport's popularity was the ease with which it could be practiced. A person did not need a group of teammates in order to practice the skills required by the game, nor did he (or she) require a lot of expensive equipment. It was the ideal pastime for youngsters of all ages and economic backgrounds.

Ned Irish

It was not long before the sport became popular in New York high schools and colleges. The metropolitan area became a hoops hotbed, with teams representing schools such as Fordham University, Manhattan University, Long Island University (LIU),

Basketball has long been popular in New York City. In a photo from a 1934 game, an NYU player (number 4) jumps to gain possession of the ball.

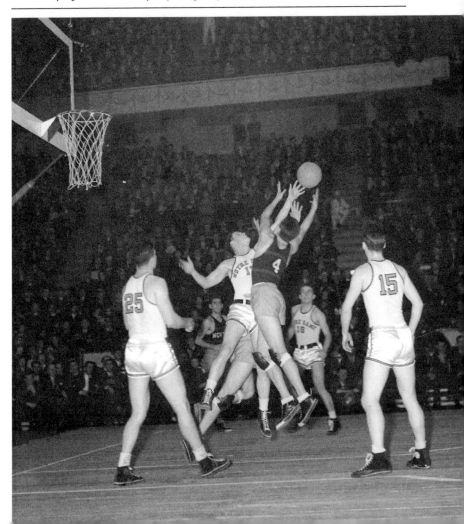

City College of New York (CCNY), St. John's University, and New York University (NYU). By the 1930s, thousands of fans were filling undersized school gyms to root for their favorite local players.

Sportswriter Edward Simmons "Ned" Irish took note of this phenomenon and came up with the idea of moving the games into New York's most famous arena, Madison Square Garden, on Eighth Avenue between Forty-ninth and Fiftieth Streets. His idea proved to be an immediate success. Over sixteen thousand fans filled the Garden to watch NYU defeat Notre Dame in Irish's first promotion on December 27, 1934. College doubleheaders soon became a staple of the Garden schedule, and the game's popularity spread across the nation.

It was only a matter of time before members of the Arena Managers Association of America—who, like Irish, controlled indoor arenas in some of the nation's larger cities—decided to try to organize the sport on a professional level. In this way, they reasoned, they could keep their arenas filled during the winter months when they would otherwise remain unoccupied between hockey games. On Thursday, June 6, 1946, these owners met to form the Basketball Association of America (BAA). With Ned Irish as owner, the New York Knickerbockers came into existence, bringing professional basketball to the Big Apple.

It took the Knicks—and pro basketball—several years to surpass the college game in popularity in New York. The team eventually developed a loyal following that reveled in the club's success in the early 1970s when it won a pair of championships. Despite its failure to follow up those great teams with another title since then, the club continues to play to full houses in Madison Square Garden, the world's most famous arena.

CHAPTER 1

An NBA Institution

The New York Knickerbockers are one of the oldest franchises in the National Basketball Association (NBA). They played in the first game in the history of the Basketball Association of America (the NBA's forerunner) back in 1946. In over a half-century of play, the Knicks have won two championships. The teams of the early 1970s exhibited a high degree of teamwork and unselfishness that is desired, but rarely found, in the modern game. The club developed a legion of loyal fans who dream of re-capturing the glory of those championship teams.

The Basketball Association of America

When the members of the Arena Managers Association of America met in New York's Hotel Commodore in June of 1946, they formed the brand new 11-team Basketball Association of America. The clubs were separated into two divisions, with the Knicks joining the Boston Celtics, Philadelphia Warriors, Providence Steamrollers, Washington Capitols, and Toronto Huskies in the East. The West comprised the Chicago Stags, Cleveland Rebels, Detroit Falcons, Pittsburgh Ironmen, and St. Louis Bombers.

Each team paid a $10,000 franchise fee, with the money going to cover the league's operating expenses. Chief among these was the salary of Maurice Podoloff, former president of the American Hockey League, who agreed to become the first president of the BAA.

The Original Knicks

In order to build on the existing college basketball fan base, the BAA clubs recruited many players who had starred in their geographical regions in college. Those who graced the first New York roster in 1946–47 included Sid "Sonny" Hertzberg (the first Knicks captain) and Hank Rosenstein of CCNY, Ralph Kaplowitz (the first player to sign) of NYU, Ossie Schectman of LIU, and Dick Murphy of Manhattan. They were joined by other local products: Nat Militzok out of Hofstra and Cornell, Tom Byrnes of Seton Hall in neighboring New Jersey, and Leo "Ace" Gottlieb,

Leo "Ace" Gottlieb (number 9, right) and Ralph Kaplowitz (number 5) reach for a rebound in a 1946 game against the Detroit Falcons.

a New Yorker who had not played college ball. Stan Stutz of Rhode Island State and Forest Weber of Purdue (the tallest and oldest player on the team) were the non–New Yorkers who rounded out the cast.

The clubs had an unofficial salary cap of approximately $50,000 per ten-man team. In New York, Kaplowitz signed for a high of $6,500. The Knicks' coach was Neil Cohalan, another New York product who had been head coach at Manhattan for 13 years. He signed a one-year contract with the understanding that Joe Lapchick, who was finishing out his term as coach of St. John's, would take over the reins the following year.

Since Madison Square Garden already had a crowded schedule of hockey and college basketball games, the Knicks were forced to play many of their home games at the Sixty-ninth Regiment Armory, another local arena. They would continue to split home games between the two arenas through 1960.

With the city so enchanted by the college game, owner Irish did everything he could to draw attention to his new pro squad. Since television was in its infancy, he was prepared to pay radio station WHN to broadcast the team's games. As announcer Marty Glickman recalled, "Ned asked [WHN general manager] Bert Lee, 'How much will it cost me to have our games on WHN?' And Bert said, 'Not only will it cost you nothing but we'll pay you $250 a game.'"[1]

The First Games

On November 1, 1946, the Knicks took the court to play the Toronto Huskies at Toronto's Maple Leaf Gardens in the first game in BAA history. Paced by Gottlieb's 14 points, the New Yorkers won by a score of 68–66 before a crowd of 7,090 fans.

The contest generated sufficient attention that a near-sellout crowd of 17,205 turned out at the Garden for the Knicks' first home game against the Chicago Stags. Although New York lost in overtime, 78–68, the game was well received. As the *New York Times* reported in the next day's edition,

> This being a play-for-pay circuit, it was most gratifying to those concerned that 17,205 spectators were on hand for the home debut of the Knickerbockers. Then there was a stirring regulation wind-up that saw Ossie Schectman, former

LIU star, hit the target with a one-handed toss just thirty-five seconds before time ran out. This desperate shot brought about a 64–64 deadlock and, with the seconds ticking away, necessitated a five-minute overtime period, the first in the league.

The crowd, which between halves had been treated to a fur fashion show and an abbreviated basketball exhibition, in which the Original Celtics . . . played a 1–1 tie with a team composed of New York Football Giants, was thrilled.[2]

The Knicks got off to a 10–2 start and finished their first season with a record of 33–27, good for third place in the six-team East. The sport's popularity in New York enabled the team to

Dick McGuire and Carl Braun leap over teammates for a publicity photo in 1955. During the 1950s, the Knicks made the playoffs for nine consecutive seasons.

draw more than 100,000 fans, making them one of only two clubs to surpass that mark in the league's maiden season.

Molding a Winner

Lapchick replaced Cohalan as coach the following year. Over the next two seasons, he guided the team to 26 and 32 victories. In the summer of 1949, the BAA merged with the older National Basketball League (NBL) and rechristened itself the National Basketball Association (NBA).

In addition to a new coach, the Knicks also added several new players. Among those who played significant roles were Carl Braun, a former pitcher in the New York Yankees farm system, who would lead the team in scoring from 1947–48 to 1949–50; six-foot, six-inch-tall Harry Gallatin, the team's top draft pick in 1948, who took over in the pivot (a position to the side or near the top of the free throw line usually taken by the center); Dick McGuire, who quickly became one of the league's top playmakers; and Ernie Vandeweghe, who played for the Knicks while attending medical school.

The result was a team that would make the playoffs for nine consecutive years. Although they never won a championship in that time, the Knicks made the finals for three straight years, twice narrowly missing a title.

Two Near Misses

In 1950–51, the Knicks met the Rochester Royals for the title. Rochester won the first three games, but the Knicks bounced back to take the next three to even the series. With Game 7 tied and less than a minute to go in regulation time, Rochester guard Bob Davies sank a pair of free throws, and the Royals went on to a 79–75 victory.

The following season, the Knicks met the Minneapolis Lakers in the finals. New York again lost in seven games, after dropping the opener on a freak play. Late in the second period, Al McGuire (Dick's brother) was fouled in the act of shooting. The ball went in, but, amazingly, neither of the two officials had been looking at the basket. Rather than getting two and possibly three points, New York was forced to settle for one when McGuire made one of the two foul shots. Regulation time ended with the teams tied, and the Royals won in overtime. Had the basket counted, the Knicks might well have won, quite possibly changing the outcome of the series, which was taken by Minneapolis, four games to three.

The Knicks reached the finals again in 1952–53. This time, they lost to George Mikan and the Lakers in only five games. New York finished above .500 in each of the next two seasons, but despite the addition of players such as Richie Guerin, Kenny Sears, and Willie Naulls, the team fell short in the playoffs both times.

Hard Times

The Knicks' success in the early 1950s—together with the effects of a college basketball point-shaving scandal in 1951—attracted many Metropolitan area basketball fans to the pro game. By the end of the decade, however, the team had begun to fall on hard times. Although the club retained many of the same players, it could not find a big man to match up against superstars like Bill Russell and Wilt Chamberlain at the center position. The Knicks fell into the NBA East basement, and Lapchick was succeeded in turn by Vince Boryla, Fuzzy Levane, and Carl Braun without much effect.

The decade of the 1960s did not bring any immediate improvement. Although the 1959–60 squad averaged a franchise-high 117.3 points per game, its record was just 27–48. The next year, the team won just 21 of 79 games. One of the losses was a 162–100 thrashing at the hands of the Syracuse Nationals—the worst loss in franchise history.

Powered by Guerin's team-record 2,303 points, the 1961–62 Knicks improved to 29–51. The next year, however, they sank to the bottom of the standings. They finished with a 21–59 record, for the lowest winning percentage (.263) in team history. On March 2, 1962, they played in one of the most famous games in NBA annals. That night, New York lost to the Philadelphia Warriors, 169–147, in a game played in Hershey, Pennsylvania. Although three Knicks scored 30 or more points, the star of the game was Wilt Chamberlain of the Warriors, who poured through an NBA-record 100 points. The team's weakness at center was never more evident.

Help, however, was just around the corner.

Foundation of a Champion

After another poor showing in 1963–64, the Knicks began to improve themselves through productive use of the draft. Their key selection was six-foot, nine-inch center Willis Reed from Grambling University with the second pick in 1964. Reed gave New York a presence it had been lacking. He had an immediate impact and became the first Knick ever to win Rookie of the Year honors. Together with fellow rookies Jim Barnes and Howard Komives, Reed helped New York improve its record to 31–49.

Rookie Dick Van Arsdale joined the club the next season, as did sharp-shooting guard Dick Barnett, who came over in a trade

Wilt Chamberlain became the first NBA player to score 100 points in a single game, a record that still stands today, in a 1962 game against the Knicks.

with the Lakers. In an effort to add even more size to the team, the Knicks also acquired six-foot, eleven-inch center Walt Bellamy from the Baltimore Bullets. That deal, however, did not work out as planned. Although he was a proficient scorer, Bellamy's defense left much to be desired. Even more importantly, his acquisition forced the team to move Reed to forward, where he was not as effective.

In 1966–67, the Knicks selected Michigan's Cazzie Russell as the first overall pick in the draft, and the team made it to the postseason playoffs for the first time since 1959. The following year, three more important pieces were added to the puzzle. Walt Frazier was drafted out of Southern Illinois University. Bill Bradley joined the team after spending two years in England, where he had been attending Oxford University as a Rhodes scholar. The man who molded the pieces into a functioning unit was Red Holzman, who took over as head coach in late December after the team got off to a 15–22 start under Dick McGuire (who had held the position since the 1965–66 season). The Knicks immediately responded to Holzman's defense-conscious philosophy. They won 28 of their final 45 games to give the team its first winning season since 1958–59.

The Trade

One problem that had to be addressed was Bellamy's failure to fit into Holzman's defensive scheme. The issue was resolved on December 19, 1968, when the Knicks acquired forward Dave De-Busschere from the Detroit Pistons in exchange for Bellamy and Komives. In addition to getting one of the league's foremost defensive forwards, the deal also allowed the Knicks to move Reed back to the center position, where he was most comfortable, thereby improving the club at two positions. As Holzman later said, "We made some great trades, but this one has to be considered the best. That made us a great team."[3]

Inspired by DeBusschere, the Knicks won 36 of their last 47 games (they had been 18–17 before the trade). They led the league in defense, allowing just 105.2 points per game. In the playoffs, they swept Eastern Division champion Baltimore in four games before losing to the Boston Celtics in the division semifinals.

New York fans took the team into their hearts. They appreciated the way the players performed as a unit, combining a smothering defense with pinpoint passing and accurate shooting. Many fans in New York looked forward to the coming season with high expectations.

A Pair of Championships

Everything came together for the Knicks in 1969–70. They won 9 of their first 10 games and set an NBA record by winning 18 straight games from October 24 through November 28. For the season, they parlayed a pressure defense and selfless passing game into a 60–22 record and an Eastern Division title.

In the playoffs, New York defeated Baltimore in an exciting seven-game first-round series. They then steamrolled past the

Dave DeBusschere (left) fights for the ball with Wilt Chamberlain of the L.A. Lakers in a 1970 playoff game. The Knicks bested the Lakers to win their first championship title.

Milwaukee Bucks and Kareem Abdul-Jabbar in 5 games to reach the NBA finals, where their opponent was the Los Angeles Lakers team of Wilt Chamberlain and Jerry West. The exciting matchup ended with Reed making a dramatic comeback from a leg injury to lead the Knicks to victory in Game 7 to give the Knicks the first title in team history.

The following season, the Knicks again topped the Eastern Division. After beating the Atlanta Hawks in the opening round of the playoffs, however, they were defeated by the Bullets in another exciting seven-game series, ending their dreams of a second consecutive crown.

An early-season trade with Baltimore brought flashy guard Earl Monroe to New York in 1971, giving the team more scoring punch. It took a while for him to modify his game to fit New York's philosophy, but by playoff time, the Knicks had come together as a team. They breezed past Baltimore and Boston before losing to the Lakers in the finals, four games to one.

The Knicks won their second NBA championship the following year. They finished the 1972–73 regular season with a 57–25 mark, good for second place behind Boston in the Atlantic Division. For the second straight year, they beat Baltimore and Boston in the early rounds of the playoffs, then faced Los Angeles in the finals. This time, however, they reversed the pattern of the previous year. They dropped Game 1 to the Lakers, then swept the next four contests to take the title. The Knicks' pressing defense held Los Angeles to less than 100 points in each of their four victories. Unbeknownst to New York fans, it would be 21 years before the team would make it back to the finals.

The Lean Years

New York managed to win 49 games in 1973–74, but Reed's retirement following the end of the season marked the beginning of a period of mediocrity for the team. The Knicks dropped below the .500 mark in 1974–75 for their first losing season in eight years. The team's veteran players were beginning to show signs of aging, and the results could be seen in the standings. After two more losing seasons, Holzman retired. He was replaced as head coach by Reed, who guided the club to a 43–39 record in 1977–78.

By this time, Bob McAdoo had been acquired from the Buffalo Braves to provide offensive help. He led the team in scoring for three straight years. The club needed much more than McAdoo, however, and when it got off to a 6–8 start in 1978–79, Reed was fired. Holzman returned as coach in an attempt to help the team recapture the magic of the early 1970s.

Such was not to be, however. The club added players like Micheal Ray Richardson, Ray Williams, and Bill Cartwright through the draft, but the chemistry was not right. In Holzman's four seasons, the Knicks posted just one winning record (1980–81). He finally stepped down for good in 1982 and was replaced by Hubie Brown.

The Knicks bounced back under Brown, posting winning records in each of his first two seasons at the helm. The star of the team was hometown hero Bernard King, who came to the Knicks in a trade with the Golden State Warriors. In 1983–84, King averaged 26.3 points per game, the fifth best mark in the league. On January 31 and February 1, he had back-to-back 50-point games against the San Antonio Spurs and Dallas Mavericks.

King averaged an incredible 42.6 points per game in the Knicks' five-game first-round playoff series win over the Detroit Pistons. New York then lost to the eventual NBA-champion Boston Celtics in seven games in the Eastern Conference semifinals. For his accomplishments that season, King was named to the All-NBA First Team.

Bernard King, a New York native, became the Knicks' star player in the early 1980s.

The following year, King was even better. On Christmas Day 1984, he scored 60 points against the New Jersey Nets for a new club record. Later that season, he set another team mark by scoring 20 or more points in 24 consecutive games. On March 23, however, his season came to a premature end when he tore the anterior cruciate ligament in his right knee. He finished as the first Knick ever to lead the league in scoring, notching 32.9 points per game.

The Luck of the Draw

Despite King's heroics, the Knicks were struggling as a team. They finished the 1984–85 season with a 24–58 record. The team's poor performance earned it a spot in the NBA's first draft lottery for the seven teams that failed to make the playoffs. With the odds stacked against them, the Knicks won the draw, giving them the first overall pick in the 1985 college draft. With that pick, they selected Patrick Ewing, Georgetown University's seven-foot, All-American center.

Ewing started the pros with a bang, winning Rookie of the Year honors in 1985–86. It was not until two years later, however, that the Knicks began to show significant signs of improvement. By that time, Rick Pitino had been hired as coach. In 1987–88, Pitino and Ewing led the Knicks back into the postseason with the help of Rookie of the Year guard Mark Jackson.

For the 1988–89 season, the Knicks added rugged forward Charles Oakley in a trade with the Chicago Bulls. Oakley's rebounding skills blended in well with Pitino's fast-paced attack. The result was the club's first Atlantic Division title since 1970–71 and its best record since the championship season of 1972–73. In the playoffs, however, the Knicks' drive to the crown was short-circuited in the conference semifinals by the Chicago Bulls, led by Michael Jordan.

Prior to the start of the next season, Pitino gave up control of the team to return to the college ranks as head coach at the University of Kentucky. He was replaced by Stu Jackson, who led the team to a third-place finish in 1989–90. After one more year of mediocrity, Knicks fortunes took a dramatic turn for the better when Dave Checketts was named club president on March 1, 1991.

The Riley Era

One of Checketts's first moves was to name Pat Riley as the team's head coach. Riley had led the Lakers to nine Pacific Division titles and four NBA championships in nine years as coach of the team. With a career winning percentage of .733 (the best in league history), many people thought he was just the man to help the Knicks return to prominence.

The Knicks responded to Riley's no-nonsense approach by winning 51 games in 1991–92 and 60 the next season. The club played tenacious defense and scored just enough points to win. In the playoffs, however, they could not get past the Bulls either year. When Michael Jordan announced his retirement prior to the 1993–94 season, the Knicks seemed poised to replace the Bulls as league champions. Unfortunately, such was not to be the case.

Following a 57–25 mark in the regular season, New York defeated the New Jersey Nets and the Bulls to reach the NBA finals. Their opponents were the Western Conference–champion Houston Rockets, led by center Hakeem Olajuwon. In a hard-fought series dominated by the defenses, the two clubs battled through seven games without either team scoring 100 points in a game. The Knicks led, three games to two, but Houston won the final two contests to take the championship.

The Knicks bounced back in 1994–95, posting a 55–27 record, the second best in the Eastern Conference. After defeating the Cleveland Cavaliers in the opening round of the playoffs, they faced Reggie Miller and the Indi-

Pat Riley's no-nonsense approach to coaching brought the Knicks to several postseason series.

ana Pacers in the conference semifinals. The tone for the series was set in the very first game. Miller scored 8 points in the final 16 seconds to wipe out a five-point New York lead and give Indiana the victory. The Knicks gamely fought back but were ultimately eliminated in 7 exciting games.

The defeat was particularly hard for Riley to swallow. He resigned the day after the playoffs ended and was replaced by veteran NBA coach Don Nelson. Nelson lasted less than one season in the position. He was replaced by longtime assistant coach Jeff Van Gundy, who led the team into the new millennium.

Another Trip to the Finals

The Knicks played competitive ball under Van Gundy, posting a winning record in each of his seasons. With Larry Johnson and Allan Houston joining veterans Ewing, Oakley, and John Starks, the team compiled a 57–25 mark—the third best in franchise history—in Gundy's first full season as head coach (1996–97). New York looked ready to make a run at the Bulls but never got the chance. In the conference semifinals against the Miami Heat (now coached by Pat Riley), the Knicks held a commanding lead of three games to one. The Heat swept the next three games, however, ending the Knicks' season in disappointing fashion.

Marcus Camby dunks the ball in a 1999 playoff game against the Indiana Pacers. Camby helped the Knicks beat the Pacers in six games.

Despite a wrist injury to All-Star center Ewing, the Knicks again made it back to the playoffs in 1997–98. After gaining a measure of revenge by upsetting the Heat in the opening round, they lost in the conference finals to the Pacers.

With age catching up to some of the team's stars, the Knicks sent Starks and Oakley packing in deals that brought Latrell Sprewell and Marcus Camby to New York. The team managed to qualify for the playoffs as the eighth and last seed in the Eastern Conference with a 27–23 mark in the strike-shortened 1998–99 season.

The postseason, however, was a whole other story. Playing top-seeded Miami in the first round, the Knicks pulled off a stunning upset by beating the Heat in 5 games. They then swept the Atlanta Hawks in 4 games to advance to the conference finals. In a hard-fought six-game matchup, the Knicks made their way past the Pacers to become the first number eight seed in league history to reach the NBA finals. There, with center Patrick Ewing sidelined with a partially torn tendon, the Knicks' valiant run finally came to an end. Tim Duncan and David Robinson carried the San Antonio Spurs to their first NBA title, defeating New York in 5 games.

Rebuilding

The Knicks playoff run in 1998–99 marked their transformation from a half-court team built around the aging Patrick Ewing to a more athletic club led by Sprewell, Houston, and Camby. At age 37, Ewing had enough left to help the Knicks to the conference finals again in 1999–2000, but it was becoming obvious to most observers that the Knicks could not win another title with an offense built around him.

New York slipped to third place in the Atlantic Division in 2000–01 and then lost to the Toronto Raptors in the first round of the playoffs. Prospects for the immediate future did not appear bright. Many of the players were earning exorbitant salaries, which made them difficult to trade. Moreover, salary cap problems limited the team's ability to pursue free agents who might be able to help them.

Shortly after the start of the 2001–02 season, Van Gundy resigned as coach. The Knicks struggled under his replacement, Don Chaney, and missed the playoffs for the first time in 15 years. It remains to be seen how long it will take them to regain their place among the league's elite. New York fans will always have memories of the 1970s, however, as a reminder of a time when their heroes showed the country how the City Game was meant to be played.

CHAPTER 2

Willis Reed

Willis Reed broke into the NBA with a bang, winning the Rookie of the Year award in 1965 as a center. He went on to enjoy a ten-year career as the inspirational leader of the Knicks, helping New York to two championships. In 1970, he became the first player ever to be selected Most Valuable Player for the regular season, the All-Star Game, and the playoffs in the same season.

A Rural Childhood

Willis Reed Jr. was born on June 25, 1942, on his grandparents' farm outside of tiny Hico, Louisiana. As he later joked, "Hico is so small, it doesn't have any population."[4] His father, Willis Sr., was a truck driver who entered the army to serve in World War II three weeks after Willis's birth. The job of raising the youngster was left to his mother, Inell, who lived on the farm along with her eleven brothers and sisters.

When young Willis was three years old, his father returned from the war. The family eventually moved to nearby Bernice, where Willis Sr. worked for Lindsey Bonded Warehouse. His wife took on odd jobs while the younger Reed helped out by mowing lawns and picking cotton.

By the time Willis was in the eighth grade, he had saved enough money to buy himself a bicycle. Unfortunately, he fell off it while riding one day and broke his left arm. This forced the natural left-hander to develop some dexterity with his right hand, which helped him in his later years as a basketball player.

When Willis entered Elliott High School as a ninth-grader, he stood six feet, five inches tall. He bought himself a basketball hoop, which he attached to a pole in his backyard. Willis was not a natural athlete, and his clumsiness and awkwardness made him the butt of many jokes at school. "I wasn't good," he wrote in his book *The View from the Rim*, "but I was big."[5] He also had a violent temper and constantly got into fights.

At Elliott, Willis came under the influence of Lendon Stone, who coached the baseball, basketball, and football teams. Stone helped him develop into an all-state end in football, but thought

Willis Reed poses for an action shot. Reed was drawn to basketball because of his size.

he had even more potential in basketball. By his junior year, Willis felt the same way. "After the tenth grade," he said, "I felt like I had some purpose. My future was in basketball. I liked football and I played it, but basketball was for me."[6]

Around this same time, Willis transferred to West Side High School, a new school with better athletic facilities. Stone also went to West Side as basketball coach, and the two led the school to the state Class A basketball championship in Willis's senior year of 1960.

That year, Willis came into his own as a player, scoring an amazing 1,184 points. He did not neglect his studies, either, and when he graduated that June, he did so as an honor student and vice president of his class. In recognition of his achievements on the court, his basketball uniform number, 22, was retired.

A Small-College Star

Willis was recruited by many colleges and eventually accepted a scholarship to Grambling State University, a black school located in Ruston, Louisiana. The university's basketball coach, Fred Hobdy, had helped recent graduate Bob Hopkins make it to the NBA, and Reed hoped Hobdy could do the same for him.

The summer before he entered Grambling, Reed worked out with Howard Willis, Grambling's graduating center. He taught Reed how to play the physical style of the game he would face in college, where more pushing and shoving was allowed than at the high-school level. The youngster still had much to learn and began his freshman season as a reserve. Reed began to doubt himself as a player and even considered quitting school. Willis, however, helped convince him to stay. The two continued to work out together, and by the time Grambling was ready to play its first Southwestern Athletic Conference (SWAC) game, Reed was the starting center. In that first game as a starter against Southern University, the six-foot, nine-inch Reed gave a preview of what he was capable of by scoring 20 points and grabbing 21 rebounds.

By the end of his freshman season, Reed was averaging just under 21 points per game. He helped Grambling to a 27–4 record and a spot in the postseason National Association of Intercollegiate Athletics (NAIA) Tournament, the small-college equivalent of the National Collegiate Athletic Association (NCAA) Tournament. There, Grambling won all five of its games to take the championship. Reed was one of the first freshmen ever named to the all-tournament team.

The Tigers returned to the NAIA tournament in Reed's junior year. This time they lost in the semifinals to Pan American College. The following season, Grambling again reached the tourney, with Reed leading the team in scoring (26.6 points per game) and rebounding (21.2 per game). However, the Tigers were upset in the second round and Reed's college career came to an end. In four seasons, he helped Grambling compile a 108–17 record. Reed was named an NAIA All-American in each of his last two years and was inducted into the NAIA Hall of Fame in 1970.

Following his graduation in 1964, Reed was invited to try out for the U.S. Olympic team, which would be competing that year in Tokyo, Japan. Despite playing well, he was not chosen for the squad. As he later recalled, "I went away convinced that I hadn't played well enough to make the team and others had, but I think now it was more a lack of people who knew what they were doing. . . . At that time they didn't think these [black] schools in the south produced basketball players. To me, it was just one of many realizations that you don't always get what you deserve."[7]

Another Slight

Reed had been followed by many NBA scouts during his years at Grambling. Red Holzman of the New York Knickerbockers was especially impressed by Reed's progress as a player. "He kept getting bigger, stronger and better all the time," recalled Holzman. "He could move and run, too, for such a big guy."[8]

The Knicks were also interested in Texas Western University's All-American center Jim "Bad News" Barnes. Because Barnes had played in a major college program, New York decided to take him with its first pick in the May 1964 college draft. They then selected Reed with the first pick of the second round. Believing he had been slighted because of his small-college background, Reed signed a $14,000 contract, determined to prove that he should have been taken ahead of Barnes.

Rookie of the Year

The Knicks originally figured Barnes would be their starting center, with Reed either backing him up or playing forward. With Barnes playing with the Olympic team in Tokyo, however, Reed had a chance to show what he could do. By the time Barnes joined the team, Reed had won the starting center job. Barnes began the year at forward.

Reed became the first member of the Knicks to be named NBA Rookie of the Year. Here, he drives past Wilt Chamberlain to score in a finals game.

Reed had impressed coach Eddie Donovan at the very beginning of training camp when he asked him for a copy of the rule book to study. As Reed explained, "I want to know what I can do and what I can't do up here."[9] No player had ever made such a request of the coach.

As the season progressed, Reed continued to impress observers. In a game against the Los Angeles Lakers in March, he scored 46 points, the second highest single-game total ever posted by a Knicks rookie. For the year, he finished seventh in the league in scoring (19.5 points per game) and fifth in the league in rebounding (14.7 per game). His 1,175 rebounds were also a new team single-season record, surpassing the mark set by Harry Gallatin, who had taken over as coach in the middle of the year.

Along with fellow rookies Barnes, Howard Komives, and Emmette Bryant, Reed helped the club to a nine-game improvement in the standings. He also made the first of his seven All-Star Game appearances. For his efforts, he became the first Knick ever named NBA Rookie of the Year. For the first time in many years, New York basketball fans had reason to be optimistic about the future.

Leader of the Knicks

The Knicks continued to improve the makeup of the team in 1965. Dave Stallworth and Dick Van Arsdale were added through the draft, and Dick Barnett by way of a trade with the Lakers. The team also picked up center Walt Bellamy from the Baltimore Bullets. This move disappointed Reed, who was asked to switch to forward to make room for Bellamy. He did so without complaint, but the results were not as positive as expected. Reed's performance was hindered by a foot injury that required surgery after the season. He was still named to the All-Star Game, however, becoming the first player in league history to be honored as both a center and a forward.

The following season, Dick McGuire replaced Gallatin as coach. In the team's home opener, the Knicks faced the Los Angeles Lakers. The game was a rough one. Toward the end of the third quarter, Lakers forward Rudy LaRusso suddenly punched Reed in the jaw. Reed had made every effort to control his temper since he had been in the league, but this was too much for him to ignore. "I guess I just lost my head," he said later, "but I struck out at anything in a blue uniform."[10] When the fight was over, Reed was ejected from the game. The Lakers, however, came out on the short end as LaRusso, center Darrell Imhoff, and forward John Block all felt the results of Reed's wrath. LaRusso was pummeled by Reed's punches, Imhoff was knocked down and required stitches over his eye, and Block suffered a broken nose. Few players would ever challenge him again.

The Knicks finished the year by making the playoffs for the first time since 1959. Although they lost to the Boston Celtics in the first round, they showed signs of greatness. In Reed, the players found their leader, someone who sacrificed personal glory for the good of the team. His ability to lead by example was recognized by Knicks management and he was named the team's captain prior to the start of the 1967–68 season. The move proved to be as beneficial to Reed as it was to his teammates. "Becoming captain helped me to handle my anger," said Reed. "Once you get to be captain, you become a key man. People look at you. You can't expect players to react other than the way I react. . . . Now I feel I must set an example, show that I have maturity."[11]

With Walt Frazier and Bill Bradley joining the team, the Knicks' prospects looked good. A disappointing start, however, caused McGuire to return Reed to center to reorganize the club. New York responded by winning seven of its next eight games, including a victory over the Lakers in which Reed scored a career-high 53 points. Since the Knicks could not afford to keep Bellamy and his salary on the bench, Reed eventually returned to forward. It became obvious, however, that his future was at the center position.

McGuire was fired when the Knicks' record fell to 15–22. He was replaced by New York scout Red Holzman. Holzman began to turn the team around by stressing defense and teamwork, the cornerstones of Reed's game. The Knicks finished the 1967–68 season with a mark of 43–39, their first winning season since 1959. Even a first-round playoff defeat at the hands of the Philadelphia 76ers could not get the team down. The young club knew it was headed in the right direction.

The Reed-Bellamy issue was settled once and for all on December 19, 1968. On that day, Bellamy was traded to the Detroit

Pistons, together with guard Howard Komives, for forward Dave DeBusschere. Reed received news of the deal with open arms. "Coming back to center," he said, "is like coming home. It's like being in a foreign country for a long time and then coming back to your old home town."[12]

He responded with the finest year of his career, averaging 21.1 points per game and grabbing a career-high 1,191 rebounds. Injuries to forwards Phil Jackson and Cazzie Russell, however, derailed the team's playoff hopes. After sweeping the Baltimore Bullets in the opening round, New York lost to the Celtics in the division finals.

A Season to Remember

Prior to the 1969–70 season, Reed signed a new three-year contract calling for yearly salaries of $125,000, $150,000, and $175,000. He proved he was worth every penny the following season.

The Knicks broke from the gate quickly by winning their first five games. After a loss to San Francisco, the team proceeded to put together an NBA-record eighteen-game winning streak, with Reed leading the way. With the Knicks in first place, teammates Reed, Frazier, and DeBusschere were named to the All-Star squad. Reed scored 21 points and pulled down 11 rebounds to pace the East to a 142–135 victory. For his efforts, he was named the game's Most Valuable Player.

Despite suffering from stomach spasms and an assortment of other nagging injuries, Reed finished the year averaging a

Knicks captain Willis Reed celebrates the club's first NBA championship in 1970 following Game 7 against the L.A. Lakers.

career-high 21.7 points per contest. For his role in helping the Knicks to a 60–22 record during the regular season, he was voted the league's Most Valuable Player, the first Knick ever so honored.

By the time the playoffs began, Reed was receiving injections of cortisone to reduce the pain in one of his knees. Somehow, he was still able to hold his own against centers Wes Unseld (Baltimore Bullets) and Kareem Abdul-Jabbar (Milwaukee Bucks) as the Knicks won their first two playoff series to move into the NBA finals against the mighty Los Angeles Lakers and seven-foot, two-inch Wilt Chamberlain.

The Knicks and Lakers split the first 4 games. Early in Game 5, Reed drove toward the basket and suddenly went down in a heap. He had injured the rectus femoris muscle in his hip and was through for the night and possibly the series. The Knicks managed to win the game but were soundly defeated in Game 6, 135–113, with Reed out of action. The Knicks were faced with the prospect of having to win a deciding Game 7 to complete their dream season on a positive note.

When the Knicks came out on the Madison Square Garden court to begin their pregame warmups before Game 7, Reed remained behind in the dressing room, having his knee attended to. No one in the filled arena knew if the captain would be able to play in the most important game of the season and, arguably, the most important in the team's long history. When Reed finally made his way out to the court, the Garden erupted in a roar. As every player on the floor watched him move about, the Knicks knew they held a large psychological advantage.

New York won the opening tip, and, on the very first play, Reed scored on a jump shot. A minute later, he hit another to give the Knicks a 5–2 lead. Somehow, the crippled captain held his own against Chamberlain. He played for a total of just 27 minutes but inspired his teammates. The Knicks went on to defeat Los Angeles, 113–99, to win their first NBA championship. For his courageous, inspiring performance, Reed was named the Most Valuable Player of the playoffs. Thus, he became the first player in league history to be named MVP of the All-Star Game, regular season, and playoffs in the same year.

The End of the Line

The Knicks slipped to 52–30 in 1970–71, but Reed continued to post impressive statistics, even though he suffered from tendinitis in his left knee. In the February 2 game against the Cincinnati Royals, he pulled down 33 rebounds to tie an all-time Knicks record. He averaged 20.9 points and 13.7 rebounds per game, but the Knicks could not make it past the Bullets in the Eastern Conference finals in the playoffs.

The following season, Reed appeared in a total of just 11 games as the tendinitis persisted. He bounced back to play in 69 games in 1972–73, but the injury had taken its toll. He averaged only 11 points per contest during the regular season. In the playoffs, however, he somehow managed to play through his physical problems. He led the Knicks past the Bullets, Celtics, and Lakers to win his second championship. In the process, he

---

Red Holzman and Willis Reed pose together at Madison Square Garden in 1977, following the announcement that Reed will take over as the Knicks' head coach.

added a second NBA finals Most Valuable Player trophy to his collection.

With his knee giving him more and more trouble, Reed retired after appearing in only 19 games in 1973–74. The Knicks had no one capable of replacing him, and the team's record began to slip. In 1977–78, after Red Holzman retired, Reed was hired as the team's coach. He brought the club home in second place in the Atlantic Division with a record of 43–39. When New York got off to a 6–8 start in 1978–79, however, Reed was let go.

After the Knicks

In 1980–81, Reed served as an assistant coach at St. John's University in New York. He then accepted a position as head coach at Creighton University and remained there for 4 years. "The four years at Creighton," he would say later, "were very important to me. It gave me a chance to run a program, make my own decisions and rub shoulders with some of the greatest coaches in the game. . . . That was a tremendous experience for me."[13]

In 1985, Reed returned to the NBA as an assistant coach with the Atlanta Hawks, then the Sacramento Kings. In February 1989, he joined the New Jersey Nets as head coach in midseason. He remained in this position for just over a year before moving into the front office, where he was general manager/vice president of basketball operations from 1988 to 1996. In this role, he played an important part in building the Nets into a playoff contender in the early 1990s. Since 1996, Reed has been the team's senior vice president in charge of player development and scouting.

When Reed retired as an active player, he was in the Knicks' career top ten in nearly every category. In 1976, he became the first New York player to have his uniform number retired. Five years later, he received his sport's ultimate honor by being elected to the Naismith Memorial Basketball Hall of Fame. For all his awards and honors, however, he is perhaps best remembered as being the heart and soul of the New York Knickerbockers. His determination, desire, and leadership helped the Knicks to the only two championships in their history.

CHAPTER 3

Walt Frazier

Walt Frazier was known in basketball circles as Clyde because his 1930s-style clothes reminded a teammate of gangster Clyde Barrow. He also stole balls the way Barrow robbed banks. Frazier developed a reputation as one of the top defensive players in the NBA and helped lead the Knicks to two championships. He teamed up with Earl Monroe to form one of the most potent backcourt combinations in league history.

Growing Up in a Large Family

Walter Frazier Jr. was born in Atlanta, Georgia, on March 29, 1945. He was the oldest of nine children (two boys and seven girls) born to Walter Frazier Sr., an automobile production line worker, and his wife Eula. Because there were two Walts in the family, the youngster came to be known as June, short for Junior. Being the firstborn child, June helped out with many of the household chores. In time he learned how to change diapers, iron clothes, and cook meals. As an adult, he explained his love of solitude as compensation for the lack of privacy he had had as a child.

From the time he was very young, sports were the love of young Walt's life. He would play basketball, football, and baseball whenever he got the chance, from early morning until he went to bed at night. His basketball skills were honed on the dirt courts of the playground near his home. As he later recalled, "It's pretty tricky dribbling on dirt. It wasn't too bad when it was dry, but if it had rained, there was a mess. You had to dribble over a hole here, a gully there, uphill and downhill."[14]

From an early age, Walt always played a position of leadership, no matter what the sport. After beginning in Little League as a center fielder, he soon moved to catcher, which remained his favorite position through high school. From the time he began playing organized football games in the fourth grade, he was a

Walt "Clyde" Frazier poses in the Knicks' locker room. Frazier played a number of sports growing up and almost pursued a career in professional football.

quarterback. And in basketball, he was always the ball handler, the one who controlled his team's offense. Unlike most others who played these positions, however, he was quiet rather than loud. He led by example rather than by telling everyone else what to do.

Walt attended the all-black David T. Howard High School from the eighth grade through the twelfth. Howard had a reputation as a sports school, and Walt fit right in. As Fred Katz wrote in *Sport* magazine, "He was always quiet and shy, sportsminded and not much of a student."[15]

Walt played one year of baseball at Howard, then quit to concentrate on basketball and football. On the basketball court, he led coach George Coffey's Rams to the state tournament in both his junior and senior years as a six-foot, two-inch guard. He excelled even more so on the football field. He led Howard to the city championship game in each of his last two years, taking them to the title as a senior.

Although he starred in basketball, most observers thought Walt's future lay in football. At that time, however, black quarterbacks were rare at major colleges and nonexistent in the pros. Walt was offered football scholarships to both Indiana University and Kansas University, but knew he would have to switch positions. Rather than do so, he decided to accept a basketball scholarship from Southern Illinois University (SIU) at Carbondale.

Saluki Star

Walt entered SIU in the fall of 1963. He averaged 22.7 points per game as a guard for the Saluki freshman team that year. (A Saluki is an Egyptian hunting dog. The school selected that as its nickname since it is located in an area known as Little Egypt.) In his sophomore year, he earned second-team Little All-America honors for coach Jack Hartman's varsity squad. Unfortunately, Walt had not taken his studies seriously. He flunked several courses, became ineligible for athletics, and lost his scholarship.

Walt returned to school the following year, paying his own way. Although he could not play, he was allowed to practice with the team. It was during this time that he began to fall in love with defense. "I had to practice it day in and day out," he

recounted, "me and four other scrub-guys, never playing any offense at all for a whole year."[16]

Through hard work, Walt made up the credits he needed and
regained his eligibility for the 1966–67 season. That year, as a
starting guard, he averaged 18.2 points and 11.9 rebounds per
game while leading the Salukis to the top spot in United Press
International's ranking of small-college teams. He was named to
the first-team Little All-America squad, along with future Knicks
teammates Earl Monroe and Phil Jackson.

Following the regular season, SIU was invited to the National
Invitational Tournament in New York City. There, Walt led his
team to the title, defeating Marquette University in the championship game, by scoring 21 points, grabbing 11 rebounds, and
handing out 5 assists. "In the end," wrote Terry Bledsoe in the
Milwaukee Journal following the 71–56 victory, "it was the superb
resources tapped by Southern's Walt Frazier which turned the
tide. Frazier seemed able, as champion athletes often are, to
come up with a big play when a big play was required."[17]

Frazier was named the Most Valuable Player of the tournament. His play impressed everyone who saw him, including
Leonard Koppett of the *New York Times*. "Frazier . . . earned the
most valuable player award," wrote Koppett in the next day's pa-
per, "as much for his floor play, feeding and opportunism as for
his scoring. He is a junior, although he sat out one year and will
be eligible for pro offers this spring. From what the full quota of
pro scouts saw of him this week, he'll get some good ones."[18]

Making a Mark in the Big City

As Koppett had explained, Frazier was eligible for the 1967 college draft since his class was graduating. Having gotten married
the previous year and having recently become a father, he decided to pass up his last college season and turn pro. The Knicks
selected him with the fifth overall pick in the first round.

Frazier's pro career got off to a rocky start when he suffered a
strained ligament in the Knicks' third exhibition game and began the regular season on the bench. When he finally got to play,
the team was struggling, badly in need of a ball handler who
could control the tempo of a game. In his eagerness to con-
tribute, the rookie tried too hard to do too much. He did not be-

Frazier celebrates on his teammates' shoulders after Southern Illinois University wins the National Invitational Tournament (NIT). Frazier earned the NIT's Most Valuable Player award.

gin to hit his stride until after the All-Star Game in January. By that time, Red Holzman had taken over as coach of the team, replacing easygoing Dick McGuire.

Holzman was a disciplinarian who stressed defense and teamwork. The difference could be seen almost immediately. The team began winning and finished the season in third place in the Eastern Division. Frazier was named to the NBA All-Rookie team, based on his averages of 9.0 points, 4.2 rebounds, and 4.1 assists per game.

The next season, New York again got off to a slow start. In December, however, center Walt Bellamy and guard Howard Komives were sent to Detroit in exchange for forward Dave

DeBusschere. The trade proved to be a turning point for the team. In addition to allowing Willis Reed to return to the center position and Bill Bradley to move to his more natural forward spot, it also gave Frazier a chance to start in Komives's place. For the year, his numbers jumped to 17.5 points, 6.2 rebounds, and 7.9 assists (third in the league) per game. In 10 playoff games against the Bullets and Celtics, they improved to 21.2, 7.4, and 9.1, respectively. The third game of the series against Baltimore saw him set a Knicks playoff record with 17 assists.

For Frazier and the Knicks, however, better days were still to come.

A Record-Breaking Performance

New York got off to a fast start in 1969–70, winning its first 5 games before falling to the Warriors. The Knicks then went on to defeat by a healthy margin every team they came up against. In one of those games (on October 30 against the San Diego Rockets), Frazier scored a career-high 43 points to go along with nine assists. "He's a coach's dream,"[19] remarked San Diego coach Jack McMahon.

Later in the streak, after having won 16 games in a row, the Knicks played Atlanta with a chance to tie the league record for consecutive victories. The Western Division–leading Hawks were no match for New York. The Knicks broke the game open in the third quarter, outscoring Atlanta, 38–12. The official statistics showed the Hawks with 22 turnovers, most of them coming as a result of Frazier's defense. As Hawks coach Richie Guerin said after the game, "Frazier showed the best individual effort and the Knicks showed me the best team performance that I have ever seen. He stole everything but our sneakers."[20] Frazier had 33 points, 8 rebounds, and 15 steals.

With a chance to break the record, the Knicks traveled to Cleveland, where they took on the Cincinnati Royals on November 28. The two clubs battled back and forth, and with just 16 seconds left to play, the Royals led 105–100 and the Knicks' streak seemed about to end.

However, Reed made two free throws to cut the margin to 105–102. Cincinnati threw the ball in, but DeBusschere intercepted the pass and went in to score. On the next inbounds play,

Reed tipped the ball away and it went to Frazier. With the seconds ticking away, Frazier went up for a shot, missed, and was fouled when he got the rebound. He went to the free throw line and calmly made his two shots to give the Knicks an incredible 106–105 victory and a new record. He finished the game with 27 points, 7 rebounds, and 5 assists.

The First Championship

The Knicks finished the season with a league-leading 60–22 mark. They faced the Bullets in the first round of the playoffs, with Frazier matched up against Baltimore's fancy-shooting guard, Earl Monroe. New York came out on top, then went on to defeat the Milwaukee Bucks in the conference finals.

Prior to the start of the finals series against the Lakers, the NBA office announced the All-NBA team and All-NBA Defensive team. For his outstanding play all year, Frazier was named as a first-team guard on both clubs. He soon showed the Lakers why he was deserving of those honors.

With the series tied at three games apiece, the Knicks faced a deciding Game 7 with their captain, Willis Reed, severely hampered by a leg injury. The team looked to Frazier to pick up his game and he did not disappoint them. He hit shot after shot, played tenacious defense, and came up with several steals. At the end of the game, the Knicks had posted a 113–99 win to give them the first championship in the franchise's history. Frazier hit 12 of 17 shots and all 12 of his free throws to lead the scoring with 36 points. He also finished with 7 rebounds, 19 assists, and 4 steals. "I felt as pumped up as I ever have on a basketball court," he later said. "I always tried to hit the open man when I played, but that night I was the open man. There's no doubt that '69–70 championship team was the highlight of my career. I think of that team every day."[21] Although Reed was named the Most Valuable Player of the playoffs, there was no doubt about who had been the star of the final game.

Clyde

The 1969–70 season brought the Knicks both fame and fortune. Frazier began to get more and more attention, not only for his

Wearing flamboyant clothing, Walt Frazier stands proudly next to his Rolls Royce. Frazier was known as much for his sense of style as for his basketball skills.

play, but also for his lifestyle. His flashy attire and cool demeanor helped make him a favorite with the fans.

One day, while in Baltimore on a road trip, Frazier bought himself a wide-brimmed Italian velour hat. When teammate Nate Bowman saw it on him, he began calling him Clyde because he resembled gangster Clyde Barrow in the movie *Bonnie and Clyde*. The nickname stuck since it also fit his style of play, which was a blend of gambling and stealing.

Frazier and his Knicks teammates made defense seem glamorous. When the opposing team had the ball, the Madison Square Garden crowd broke into chants of "Dee-fense! Dee-fense!" inspiring their heroes to perform more feats of derring-do. The anticipation of what might happen began to have an effect. As Bill Bradley explained, "It's not only that Clyde steals the ball, but that he makes them think he's about to steal it, and that he can steal it any time he wants to."[22]

Frazier continued to perform his magic in 1970–71, but the Knicks lost to the Bullets in the Eastern Conference finals in their bid for a second consecutive championship. The following year, the Knicks obtained Earl Monroe, Frazier's rival from Baltimore, in a trade.

Most observers felt the Frazier-Monroe pairing would prove to be a disastrous combination since each was used to controlling the action on the court. Each was willing to put aside his own interests, however, for the good of the team. By the end of the year, they were playing together like parts of a well-oiled machine. The Knicks blew past the Bullets and Celtics in the playoffs before losing to the Lakers in the NBA finals. Frazier averaged a career-high 23.2 points per game for the year and won All-NBA first-team honors for the second of four times. He was also named to the NBA All-Defensive first team for the fourth of seven consecutive seasons.

The following year, the Frazier-Monroe duo led New York to a 57–25 record, good for second place in the Atlantic Division. With Frazier leading the way on defense, the Knicks allowed only 98.2 points per game, for the best mark in the league.

The team peaked during the playoffs, where they defeated the Bullets and Celtics to advance to the finals. Their opponent, for the third time in four years, was the Los Angeles Lakers. The Knicks dropped the opener but bounced back to take the next four games and win their second NBA title.

Good Bye to a Knicks Legend

The Knicks again led the league in defense in 1973–74 (the fifth time in six seasons) but finished second to Boston in the Atlantic Division. Frazier led the team in scoring for the fourth consecutive season but could not help them past the eventual champion, the Celtics, in the Eastern Conference finals.

When Reed retired following the season, New York fortunes took a turn for the worse. The team finished with a losing record in each of the next three years, during which Frazier's play was one of the few bright spots. Over his last three seasons with the team, his scoring average dipped from 21.5 points per game to 19.1 to 17.4, but he continued to add to his all-time Knicks record for assists. In 1975, he made his sixth All-Star

Frazier was traded to the Cleveland Cavaliers in 1977. The trade stunned and angered many New York fans.

appearance a memorable one. He scored 30 points while leading the East to a 108–102 win over the West squad. For this he was named the game's Most Valuable Player.

Just prior to the start of the 1977–78 season, the Knicks stunned New York fans by sending Frazier to the Cleveland Cavaliers as compensation for the free-agent signing of guard Jim Cleamons. Shocked by the move, Frazier reported to Cleveland, where he played three more seasons. He was hampered by injuries, however, and saw action in a total of just 66 games. After appearing in three games in 1979–80, Frazier was put on waivers. He retired as the Knicks' all-time leader in scoring (14,617 points), assists (4,791), games played (759), and minutes played (28,995).

Despite his injuries, Frazier refused to feel sorry for himself. "If this is a tragedy," he told the *New York Times*, "I wish it to everyone. I had a very successful career. I have my health, my wealth, my peace of mind. What I did is in the books."[23]

Shaking and Baking

Following his retirement, Frazier took time away from the game. He lived on St. Croix in the Virgin Islands, where he sailed his beloved trimaran (a type of sailboat with three parallel hulls). It was not long, however, before he got involved in a variety of projects, including becoming a player agent and investing in the U.S. Basketball League. In 1989, he returned to New York, taking a position as an analyst on Knicks broadcasts.

Frazier knew he would have to work hard to become a success at his new job. "I always knew I'd have to improve my vocabulary to be an effective announcer," he told *Sports Illustrated*. "So I'd practice announcing until the words became second nature."[24] He became fascinated with words and obsessed with the dictionary. He soon started using rhyming phrases such as "shaking and baking" and "swishing and dishing" as his distinctive trademark. Frazier took his love of the English language a step further. In 2001, his humorous book about words for kids, *Word Jam*, was published.

Despite his success with his latest ventures, Frazier will always be best remembered for his play on the court. The jersey of the seven-time All-Star was retired by the Knicks in 1979. Eight years later, he was inducted into the Naismith Memorial Basketball Hall of Fame. In 1996 he was honored as a member of the NBA's 50th Anniversary All-Time Team.

CHAPTER 4

Bill Bradley

Bill Bradley was destined for greatness since his days as a schoolboy basketball sensation in Crystal City, Missouri. He was an All-American at Princeton University, attended Oxford University as a Rhodes scholar, and enjoyed a successful ten-year career with the Knicks as a small forward. Following his playing days, he entered the world of politics and was elected U.S. senator from New Jersey. He is considered by many to be a leading presidential candidate in the future.

Destined for Success

William Warren Bradley was born on July 28, 1943, in Crystal City, Missouri, a small town located on the Mississippi River some thirty-five miles south of St. Louis. His father, Warren Bradley, was president of the Crystal City State Bank; his mother, Susan, was a former junior high school teacher. They instilled in their only child the values of hard work and discipline.

As a youngster, Bill displayed an aptitude for sports. As his mother told the *New York Post*, "I could tell when he was very young, three or four months old, that he had very good muscular control."[25] His interests were not limited to sports, however. His parents made sure he was exposed to a wide variety of activities, including music, language, and dance. Despite receiving all his parents' attention, young Bill was able to keep things in perspective. "His parents brought him up right," said former Princeton trainer Eddie Zanfini. "He's an only child and you get spoiled that way. But they taught him to deny himself things to give to other people."[26]

Young Bill developed a real interest in basketball when he was in elementary school. His mother put up a basket on the family garage, and Bill practiced there for hours on end. Unlike many youngsters, he did not strive to excel in sports as a means of improving his economic status. Instead, Bill did so in an effort to be accepted as "one of the guys." As he later said, "Basketball was for me the great denominator. It didn't make any difference who you were. You were able to shoot the ball and get the rebound and make the pass, or you weren't. . . . That was a way for me to prove myself to my peers."[27]

Bill Bradley laces up in the Princeton University locker room. Bradley always had the confidence of a much older player.

Bill Bradley, playing for Princeton, outjumps a Wichita State defender to shoot a basket. Bradley broke his team's freshman record by averaging 28.4 points per game.

When Bill entered Crystal City High School, he had already grown to nearly his full adult height of six feet, five inches. He had also reached a point in his life where he no longer needed his parents to motivate him. "By the time I was fourteen," he wrote in *Life on the Run*, "I had become self-motivated. Whatever raced inside me was more demanding than any pressure applied by parents or teachers."[28] Bill practiced alone in the school gym for four hours a day, perfecting every detail of the moves he had learned over the summer at former NBA star Ed Macauley's basketball camp in St. Louis. He took to heart one of the precepts preached by Macauley: "If you're not practicing, there's always somebody somewhere who *is*, and when you meet he'll beat you."[29]

Arvel Popp, Crystal City's basketball coach, inserted Bill into the varsity team's starting lineup when he was just a freshman. The youngster responded by establishing himself as arguably the best basketball player in the history of the state. Bill scored 3,066 points in his 4 years with the Hornets and was twice named to *Scholastic* magazine's All-America team (1960 and 1961).

Bill's dedication to basketball did not interfere with his academic performance. In addition to being a straight-A student, he was also a member of the National Honor Society and president of the Missouri Association of Student Councils. As one of his teammates recalled, "Everyone looked up to him. He was sort of inspirational. Basketball was one-millionth of what he could do."[30]

In his senior year, Bill received scholarship offers from dozens of colleges. He was all set to go to Duke University, but at the last minute changed his mind. He enrolled at Princeton University, an Ivy League school located in New Jersey, which only offered scholarships to students with financial need (which did not describe Bradley). Intending to pursue a career in foreign service, Bill was attracted by the University's Woodrow Wilson School of Public and International Affairs. "It came down to the education being more important than the basketball,"[31] he explained. He entered Princeton as a freshman in the fall of 1961.

One of the Greatest College Players Ever

Bradley's success on the court continued at Princeton. He led the freshman team to a 10–4 record, averaging a freshman-record 28.4 points per game. He also set a national record by sinking 57 consecutive free throws.

In Bradley's sophomore year, he was a one-man team on the varsity, scoring points, rebounding, and passing with the confidence of a much older player. He averaged 27.3 points per game—fifth highest in the nation—and was named to the All-Ivy League team and to the *Sporting News* All-America squad. The following season, his average jumped to 32.3 points per game as he was named to virtually every All-America team. In one game against Dartmouth College, he scored an Ivy League–record 51 points. Despite his scoring heroics, he was an unselfish player who made a determined effort to distribute the ball among his teammates rather than dominate the action himself.

Following Bill's junior year, he was named to the 1964 U.S. Olympic basketball team that competed in Tokyo, Japan. Despite being the youngest member of the team, Bradley impressed everyone who saw him play. As Frank Deford wrote in *Sports Illustrated*, "He was an all-court catalyst, sparking every phase of team play. . . . Bradley was the only U.S. player smart and flexible enough to convert his style to take advantage of the international rules, which so favor an aggressive offense."[32] He returned home for his senior year with a gold medal as the U.S. team defeated all of its international opponents.

Bradley led Princeton to a 32–6 record in 1964–65. In his final game for the Tigers, he scored 58 points against Wichita State. He finished his career with 2,503 points, which at the time was fourth on the all-time major college list. He was named Player of the Year by the National Association of Basketball Coaches and won the Sullivan Award as the nation's outstanding amateur athlete.

Perhaps Bradley's greatest game came against fellow All-American Cazzie Russell and the University of Michigan in the semifinals of the Eastern Collegiate Athletic Conference Holiday Festival tournament held in New York City's Madison Square Garden. Scoring 41 points and playing outstanding defense, he single-handedly led the underdog Tigers to a 75–63 lead before fouling out. With Bradley on the bench, Michigan stormed back over the last four-and-a-half minutes to steal an 80–78 victory. After the game, legendary St. John's University basketball coach Joe Lapchick raved, "I always thought that Oscar Robertson was the greatest, but Bradley is only half a step, if that, behind him. . . . Against Michigan . . . he put on the greatest one-man exhibition I've ever seen."[33]

The Rhodes Scholar

By the time Bradley graduated from Princeton, he had grown tired of the public praise that surrounded his every move. "The greater the acclaim became," he wrote, "the more certain it was that the public appetite could never be satisfied. The only way out, I thought, was to reject basketball and become a lawyer or a businessman."[34] Despite being selected in the first round of the 1965 draft by the New York Knicks as a territorial pick, Bradley decided to leave the game he loved. (In the early years of the NBA, teams tried hard to build followings among local fans. To this end, a club was allowed to take a local player as a territorial pick in place of its regular first-round selection.) He accepted a Rhodes scholarship to study politics, philosophy, and economics for two years at Oxford University in England.

For most of his time at Oxford, Bradley never even touched a basketball. One day near the end of his second year, however, he went to a gym for some exercise. As he later described it, "There I shot alone—just the ball, the basket, and my imagination. As I heard the swish and felt my body loosen into familiar movements . . . I could hear the crowd though I was alone on the floor. A feeling came over me that stirred something deep inside. I realized that I missed the game and that the law could not replace it."[35] Three weeks later, Bradley signed a four-year contract with the New York Knicks that was worth $500,000—an extraordinary amount of money for that time.

Dollar Bill

Bradley could not possibly live up to the hype and expectations that surrounded his debut in the media capital of the world, New York City. Because of the buildup and his large contract, he had already been nicknamed Dollar Bill. Many fans expected him to dominate in the pros as he had in college and to lead a Knicks turnaround (the team had finished with a losing record in each of the previous eight seasons).

Bradley's pro debut came on December 9, 1967, against the Detroit Pistons at Madison Square Garden. (His debut was delayed because he had joined the U.S. Air Force Reserve upon leaving Oxford and served on active duty for six months.) The 18,499 fans in attendance cheered his every warm-up shot while players on the visiting team turned to watch. Once the game started, Bradley proved to be mortal. He scored just eight points as the Knicks recorded another loss. As the weekly *National Observer* reported, "In his first pro game, Bradley has made mistakes. He palmed the ball several times . . . threw passes away, and missed three foul shots."[36]

Bradley was slow for an NBA guard and struggled to adjust to the pace of the pro game. He finished his rookie season of 1967–68 averaging just 8 points, 3 assists, and 2.5 rebounds for each of the 45 games in which he appeared. Still, he showed signs of being more than just an average rookie. As coach Red Holzman said, "Bradley the rookie looked like he'd been a pro for a dozen years."[37]

Bradley himself was disappointed with his performance but determined to improve. "Basketball is the one thing in my life I could always fall back on and excel at," he told Princeton roommate Daniel Okimoto. "Now a key element of my identity has been shaken and I'll see how I deal with it."[38]

He dealt with it by working even harder than before. His improvement was substantial—his scoring average jumped to 12.4 points per game for the 1968–69 season. He also increased his rebounds per game to 4.3 (from 2.5) and assists per game to 3.7 (from 3.0). The Knicks also showed significant improvement as they won 54 games, an increase of 11 over the previous season.

That Championship Season

The following year was a pivotal one in Bradley's career. Soon after the Knicks obtained rugged forward Dave DeBusschere in a trade with the Pistons, starting forward Cazzie Russell suffered a broken ankle. Bradley moved over from guard to become the other starter at forward. Where he had been much slower than other players at the guard position, he now was much quicker than the small forwards he was matched up against. Under Holzman's steady hand, the Knicks jelled as a team and won a franchise-record 60 games during the regular season.

Employing a style of ball that stressed teamwork and unselfish play, New York won over the hearts of basketball purists everywhere. Bradley was constantly moving around until he shook free from the man who was guarding him. With his teammates constantly on the lookout for the open man, he was often left unguarded for a shot or an easy layup.

The Knicks defeated the Baltimore Bullets, Milwaukee Bucks, and Los Angeles Lakers in the playoffs to give the city its first

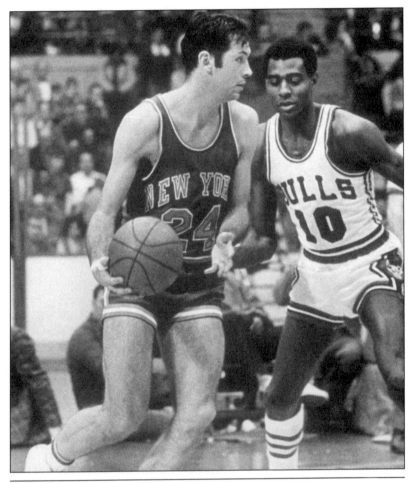

Bradley faces a Bulls player in a 1969 game. Bradley was a reliable team player, and his efforts helped the Knicks win the championship title that season.

NBA championship. Bradley averaged 14.5 points per game during the regular season. In the decisive seventh game of the NBA finals, he scored 17 points, made 5 assists, and played solid defense. As was often the case, however, he was overshadowed by the play of Walt Frazier, Dick Barnett, and Dave DeBusschere, who scored 36, 21, and 18 points, respectively.

Winning a title was everything Bradley had ever hoped and dreamed of doing. As he wrote in *Life on the Run*, "Since I was nine years old I had played basketball to become the best. Individual honors were nice but insufficient. . . . Only the NBA in the early 1970s was clearly the highest caliber in the world, and there I was part of the best team. . . . The championship vindicated my concept of and approach to the game. I had finally proved something to myself."[39]

Bradley embodied the essence of the Knicks team. He performed with a vision of how the game should be played—five players with different talents combining their skills to form a whole greater than the sum of its parts. Despite giving the appearance of calm sensibility, he would do anything he could to break his opponent's rhythm and give his team a slight edge. As Holzman recalled in *My Unforgettable Season—1970*, "He was a pest and he loved it. . . . I think everybody loved and respected Bill but he was such an irritant on the court. He could get under your skin. That's why I liked him."[40]

Back to the Top

Bradley continued his solid play over the next two seasons, averaging 12.4 and 15.1 points, but the Knicks fell short of a title each year. The Bullets gained a measure of revenge in the 1970–71 playoffs when they eliminated the Knicks in an exciting seven-game Eastern Conference finals series. The following year, the Knicks added Jerry Lucas and Earl Monroe, but it was not enough to get them past the Lakers in the NBA finals.

The Knicks bounced back to win 57 games in 1972–73, but the Celtics finished ahead of them in the Atlantic Division with an amazing 68–14 record. The two teams met in the playoffs after the Knicks dispatched Baltimore in five games in the conference semifinals. New York jumped out to a lead of three games to one, but Boston came back to tie the series at three games apiece. In the seventh game, the Knicks defense held the Celtics to 78 points (34 below their season average) to emerge victorious and advance to the NBA finals, where they would again face the Lakers.

After dropping the series opener to Los Angeles, the Knicks came back to sweep the next four games to win their second title. In the final contest, Bradley scored 20 points as New York won by a score of 102–93. It was a fitting end to the best season of his pro career, a year that saw him average a career-high 16.1 points per game and make his only All-Star appearance.

The Public Servant

Bradley played four more seasons with the Knicks, but New York never again made a serious run at a title. Bradley's scoring average dropped each season, from 14.0 to 13.3 to 11.1 to 4.3. By 1977, the team had fallen below .500, and Bradley knew it was time to move on to the next phase of his life. He retired that summer, after 10 years in the league, leaving with a career scoring average of 12.4 points per game. He was elected to the Basketball Hall of Fame in 1983, his first year of eligibility.

Unlike many other professional athletes, Bradley had prepared for his retirement while he was still an active player. He spent his off seasons traveling around, meeting new people, and visiting new places. In preparation for a career in politics, he started making contacts in Democratic circles while working as an assistant to the director of the Office of Economic Opportunity in Washington, D.C.

After retiring from basketball, Bradley set his sights on a full-time career in politics. He ran for the U.S. Senate from the state of New Jersey in 1978 and was elected with 56 percent of the vote. He was sworn in at age 35 as the youngest member of the Senate. During his 18 years in office (he was reelected in 1984 and 1990), Bradley held seats on the Finance Committee, the Energy and Natural Resources Committee, the Special Committee on Aging, and the Select Committee on Intelligence. Among his priorities were preserving the environment and improving education. He is perhaps best known for the Tax Reform

Senator Bill Bradley autographs a basketball. After retiring from playing, Bradley entered politics.

Act of 1986, which embodied many of the ideas laid out in his 1982 book, *The Fair Tax*.

Bradley left the Senate after his third term expired in 1996, satisfied with his accomplishments and looking for a new challenge. "I'm leaving the Senate," he said, "but I'm not leaving public life."[41] It soon became apparent he was planning to run for president. He did so officially in 1999, opposing Vice President Al Gore in an attempt to win the Democratic Party's nomination. Although he was unsuccessful, he is still young enough to try again in the future. Currently, Bradley is managing director of Allen & Company, Incorporated, and serves as chair of the advisory board of McKinsey & Company's Institute for the Management of Nonprofits.

Although he has been out of basketball for two-and-a-half decades, Bradley is still remembered as a starter on one of the NBA's all-time great teams. His contributions to the championship Knicks squads cannot be measured by numbers alone. His selflessness and willingness to work for the good of the team are qualities that have served him well in his post–playing career in the world of politics.

CHAPTER 5

Red Holzman

The prototypical New Yorker, Red Holzman was born in the Big Apple, went to college there, and came to prominence as the head coach of the Knicks. He guided them to the only two world championships in the franchise's long history and retired as the second winningest coach in league annals.

The New York Kid

William Holzman was born on August 10, 1920, on the Lower East Side of Manhattan. His parents, Abraham and Sophie Holzman, were Jewish immigrants. His father, a tailor, came from a small town on the Russian border, and his mother was from Romania. The couple also had two older children, a boy named Julie and a girl, Minnie.

By the time William was 4 years old, he had acquired the nickname Red because of his shock of red hair. The family moved to the Ocean Hill–Brownsville section of Brooklyn, where they lived in a tenement together with his uncle Leon and Leon's daughter, Celia. Like most city boys, Red spent most of his free time playing ball in the streets. One of his favorite hangouts was the school yard at St. Clair McEllway School. There, he could always find a game of baseball, football, basketball, soccer, or handball. Basketball quickly became his favorite.

Red's parents did not share his love of sports. They preferred that he spend his time studying so that he could do well in school. His passion could not be cooled, however, and he would often sneak out to play. "Some nights," he recalled, "in order to play at the neighborhood center I would have to throw my shoes and equipment out the back window of our apartment and then fumble around in the dark in the courtyard searching for them."[42]

Red played basketball at Junior High School 178, then continued his education at Franklin K. Lane High School, where he played on both the basketball and handball teams. While at Lane, Red also played for a fraternal organization team called the Workmen's Circle. It was there that he met his future wife, Selma Puretz, whose parents belonged to the group.

After Red graduated from Lane, he got a job working for the Local 102 union pushing a handtruck in Manhattan's garment district. On weekends he played basketball for Local 102, which had an outstanding amateur team. The five-foot, ten-inch Holzman was good enough to impress Phil Fox, one of the area referees. Fox helped him get a basketball scholarship to the University of Baltimore, where he played under coach Bucky Miller. Although Red did well at Baltimore, he was homesick for New York. After six months at the school, he transferred to the City College of New York (CCNY).

Nat Holman and the Beavers

At CCNY, Red played for one of basketball's legendary figures, Nat Holman. Known as Mr. Basketball, Holman had been a star player with the original Celtics in the 1920s, helping the club win 720 of 795 games over that time. As a coach, he stressed ball movement and defense. Many of Holzman's theories about coaching stemmed from his association with Holman.

Red learned his lessons well at CCNY. After having to sit out a year as a transfer student, he helped the Beavers to two successful seasons. Over that time, his team did not lose a single game to another metropolitan area school. Red averaged 10.9 points per

City College players hoist coach Nat Holman onto their shoulders to celebrate their NCAA title. Red Holzman learned valuable lessons while playing for Holman.

game in the 1940–41 season and 12.5 per game as a senior guard in an age when only the best players scored in double figures.

Following his graduation, Red played one season (1941–42) with the Albany club of the New York State League. The United States had recently become involved in World War II, and Holzman enlisted in the navy that summer. While stationed at the Norfolk naval base, he was able to continue to hone his skills by playing ball against other service and college teams. Playing against many of the top athletes from around the country gave Holzman's confidence a boost. By the time he got out of the service in 1945, he was ready to give pro basketball a try.

A Solid Pro

Holzman was 25 years old when he was discharged from the navy. He began playing pro ball with the New York Gothams of the American Basketball League. He was soon contacted by Fuzzy

Levane, a college friend who was playing with the Rochester Royals of the National Basketball League (NBL). In an attempt to appeal to the team's many Jewish fans, Royals owner Les Harrison had told Levane, "Get me a Jewish player. I don't care if he can play or not. Just make sure he's Jewish."[43] Levane responded by recommending Holzman.

Holzman spent his first few games glued to the Rochester bench. He finally got his chance in a game against the Sheboygan Redskins and quickly showed that he belonged in the league. He finished the 1945–46 season with the fifth best scoring average in the circuit as he led Rochester to a 24–10 record. He was named the NBL's Rookie of the Year and made the All-League first team. Holzman continued his steady play in the postseason, and the Royals went on to defeat the Fort Wayne Pistons for the league championship.

Holzman was named to the NBL All-Star team in each of his first three years. Following the 1947–48 season, Rochester, Minneapolis, Fort Wayne, and Indianapolis all left the league to join the two-year-old Basketball Association of America (BAA), a new circuit that had the backing of the owners of many of the country's hockey arenas. After the Royals' first season in the BAA, the league expanded to 17 teams and changed its name. The National Basketball Association came into existence in 1949. Rochester was one of the league's top clubs, just behind George Mikan and the Minneapolis Lakers.

It was as a member of that club that one of the highlights of Holzman's playing career came in the second game of the 1950–51 Western Division finals series against the Lakers. By that point in his career, he was no longer a regular starter. After losing to Minneapolis in the first game, however, Rochester coach Les Harrison was looking to give his team a much-needed spark. "I got an idea," he told his squad prior to the game. "Tonight I'm gonna make a change in our starting lineup. The only time we beat Minneapolis at home this season was when I started Red against them. I'm doing that again."[44]

Holzman proceeded to tally 23 points to lead both teams in scoring, as the Royals defeated the Lakers by 4 points to even the series at one game apiece. The victory helped spark Rochester past Minneapolis and into the NBA finals against the New York Knickerbockers. The Royals won the first three games of the series, but New York bounced back to take the next three to force a seventh and deciding game. In that final contest, Holzman helped the Royals to a 4-point victory, giving Rochester its first NBA championship.

A New Start

Despite having the best record in the league during the 1951–52 regular season, the Royals were defeated by the Lakers in the Western Division finals. The next year, the team did not make it past the division semifinals. After eight pro seasons, the 32-year-old Holzman knew his playing days were nearing an end.

In the summer of 1953, the Milwaukee Hawks, now coached by Holzman's old friend Fuzzy Levane, acquired the veteran guard from Rochester. Forty-six games into the new season, however, Levane was fired. Holzman was named to replace his friend. The team responded by winning 10 of its 26 games under him, not an especially good record, but better than the one compiled by Levane.

The Hawks improved to 26 wins in 1954–55 and 33 the next year as Holzman began putting into effect his theories of moving the ball, passing to the open man, and playing tough defense. In 1956–57, however, the team got off to a slow start and impatient owner Ben Kerner fired Holzman. The Hawks still finished the year with a losing record, but the groundwork laid by Holzman was beginning to pay off. It would come to fruition the following season when the Hawks won the NBA championship.

After taking a year away from the game he loved, Holzman was contacted once again by Levane, who was now a New York Knicks scout. "Red," said Levane, "you know more about the game than most coaches in the league. . . . Come down to the Garden. Be seen. We'll find a way for you to get back into basketball."[45]

Holzman took Levane's advice. The next year (1958), Levane was named the new Knicks coach. Because of Levane's recommendation, New York Knicks president Ned Irish hired Holzman as the team's chief scout. He was back working in his hometown.

Holzman coached the Milwaukee Hawks for two years, playing here in a 1954 game against the Boston Celtics, before heading back to his hometown to work for the Knicks.

Back in Charge

Holzman remained in his position as the team's chief scout for a decade. In that time, his input was instrumental in the team's drafting of players such as Willis Reed, Walt Frazier, Bill Bradley, Cazzie Russell, Phil Jackson, and Dick Van Arsdale. The club failed to fulfill its promise on the court, however, and when it got off to a 15–22 start in 1967–68, Holzman was named coach. He eagerly looked forward to the opportunity to head the team he had helped put together. As he wrote in his autobiography, "There's a time for everything in a man's life, and this, I knew, was my time, my time to do something special. And I knew I could."[46]

Holzman was determined to bring discipline to a team that had finished in fourth place in each of the previous eight seasons. He let the players know of his intentions on his very first day as coach. "This team is going to try to win a championship," he told them. "I'm going to work hard as hell and I'm going to make all of you do the same. We're going to have certain rules and those rules will be enforced."[47]

Holzman began teaching his players the theories and philosophy he had developed over his years in the game. On offense, he encouraged them to "hit the open man." Doing so ensured his team of getting a good shot and got every player involved in moving the ball around. He believed in using a set offense that required players to be in the proper positions at the proper times.

On defense, Holzman implored his players to "see the ball." This made them acutely aware of the passing lanes and where the ball was at all times. He taught them the mechanics of pressing and trapping, forcing the opposing team away from its strengths and into its weaknesses.

Holzman's methods resulted in almost immediate improvement. He lost his first 2 games at the helm before recording his first win against the reigning NBA champs, the Philadelphia 76ers. The players quickly came together as a team, and as they did so, they developed a sense of confidence in themselves and in their coach.

The Knicks compiled a 28–17 record under Holzman in 1967–68. New York finished in third place in the Eastern Division, which was the club's best finish since 1958–59. The team's successful style of play drew more and more fans to Madison Square Garden, and the team surpassed the half-million mark in home attendance for the first time in franchise history.

New York faced the Philadelphia 76ers in the playoffs, and the two teams split the first 4 games. When Walt Frazier injured his leg, however, it proved to be too much to overcome. The 76ers won the next 2 games to take the series. The future, however, was looking brighter to Knicks fans than it had in many years.

Putting It All Together

One of the reasons for the Knicks' improvement was that the players were willing to perform in specific roles for the good of the team. Willis Reed was the intimidator and Walt Frazier was the defensive wizard with lightning-quick hands. When the team traded for Dick Barnett, it got a veteran shooter in the back-court.

The move that brought everything together was the December 19, 1968, deal that sent Walt Bellamy and Howard Komives to the Detroit Pistons in exchange for forward Dave DeBusschere. DeBusschere was another fierce rebounder who was also a strong defensive player and a good shooter. Just as importantly, the trade allowed Reed to move back to his natural center position, where he was a big improvement defensively over the much less aggressive Bellamy. In addition, it opened up a spot at forward for Bradley, who was often overmatched by much quicker players at guard.

The Knicks went on to compile a 54–28 record in 1968–69, the fourth best in the league. They swept past the Baltimore Bullets in the Eastern Division semifinals, a particularly satisfying victory, since the Bullets had intimated beforehand that they preferred playing the Knicks rather than anyone else in the first round of the playoffs. New York's season finally came to an end when they were defeated by the eventual champion, the Boston Celtics, in an exciting Eastern Division finals matchup.

Championship Seasons

New York basketball fans were coming out in record numbers to see their new heroes. The 1968–69 club set a regular season home attendance mark and became the first NBA team in history to play before a million fans. They would be rewarded for their loyalty the next year.

The 1969–70 Knicks got off to a blazing start, winning 23 of their first 24 games, and never looked back. They ended the season with a franchise-record 60 wins and a first-place finish in the Eastern Division. Playing the kind of fundamentally sound game that was the delight of basketball purists everywhere, the Knicks defeated the Bullets, Bucks, and Lakers in the playoffs to walk off with their first NBA championship. Captain Willis Reed's return from a serious leg injury in the seventh game of the finals was one of the most dramatic moments in the league's history. It inspired the club to victory and showed how players who were willing to put the team first could overcome adversity and accomplish whatever they put their minds to.

By the summer of 1970, Holzman had taken on the job of team general manager in addition to his coaching duties. The Knicks came up short in their attempt to repeat as champions in 1970–71, losing to Baltimore in the division finals. The next year, they made it back to the NBA finals but were downed by the Lakers, who gained a measure of revenge for their 1970 defeat.

In his job as general manager, Holzman had added guard Earl Monroe and forward/center Jerry Lucas to the team in the 1971–72 season. The two played important roles in the success of the 1972–73 squad, with Monroe teaming with Walt Frazier to form a dynamic backcourt combination and Lucas proving to be an invaluable backup to the injury-plagued Reed at center.

Holzman yells at the referees from the sideline during a playoff series. In 1970 Holzman took on the responsibilities of general manager, in addition to his coaching duties.

The Knicks finished the 1972–73 season in second place in their division, then defeated the Bullets, Celtics, and Lakers in the postseason to give the team its second NBA title. The squad embodied Holzman's theories of team defense to the extreme, allowing a league-low 98.2 points per game (the lowest average ever for a Holzman-coached team).

The Decline

Unfortunately, age and injuries were beginning to catch up with the Knicks. The team's win total dropped from 57 to 49 to 40 to 38 over the next three seasons. After finishing with a mark below .500 for the second season in a row in 1976–77, Holzman stepped down as coach to become a consultant with the team. He was replaced by Willis Reed.

Under Reed, the team finished at 43–39 in 1977–78. When Reed was fired 14 games into the 1978–79 season, Holzman was

Red Holzman retired from coaching in 1977 to become a consultant with the Knicks. He is seen here in one of his last games as a coach.

coaxed into coming back to replace him. Unfortunately, the team he inherited included many younger players who were not disciplined enough to carry out all of his instructions. The club did improve over the next two seasons from 31 wins to 39 to 50, but the chemistry of the Knicks' championship clubs was lacking. New York fell to a 33–49 record in 1981–82, and Holzman retired for good following the season. After the Knicks lost their final game to the first-place Celtics, Boston coach Bill Fitch told reporters, "Red Holzman is a great coach. If Red were sitting on my bench with my players and I was sitting on his bench with his type of players, he would have a record that matched ours."[48]

Holzman retired as the winningest coach in Knicks history. (On March 10, 1990, the team retired jersey number 613 in honor of his win total.) He stayed with the team as a consultant for the time remaining on his contract.

Honors continued to come Holzman's way. He was inducted into the Naismith Memorial Basketball Hall of Fame in 1985 and the International Jewish Sports Hall of Fame 3 years later. On November 13, 1998, Holzman died of leukemia at the age of 78. He remains the only coach to have brought an NBA championship to the city of New York.

CHAPTER 6

Patrick Ewing

Patrick Ewing was born in Jamaica and came to the United States as a youngster. In college, he led Georgetown to an NCAA title in 1984 as a seven-foot center. One of the greatest defensive centers of all time, he continued his dominating play in a long pro career. For all his success, however, he was never able to lead his team to an NBA championship.

From Kingston to Cambridge

Patrick Aloysius Ewing was the fifth of Carl and Dorothy Ewing's seven children. He was born on August 5, 1962, in Kingston, the capital and largest city on the island of Jamaica in the West Indies. He was raised in Trench Town, a poor area outside the city, where his father was a mechanic who struggled to find work and put food on the family table.

Patrick displayed a talent for art at a young age and dreamed of someday making it his career. He also enjoyed sports. Like most boys on the island, he played soccer and cricket rather than the American sports of baseball, basketball, and football. He always played goalie in soccer, the most important defensive position on the team. His proficiency at defense would later carry over into his basketball career.

When Patrick was 8 years old, his mother moved to the United States with the help of some relatives in New York City. She settled in Cambridge, Massachusetts, where she got a job working in the cafeteria at Massachusetts General Hospital. Patrick's father joined her there 2 years later and found work making hoses for a rubber company. The Ewing children arrived, singly or in pairs, over the next few years, with Patrick coming over in January of 1975.

Patrick was introduced to basketball shortly after his arrival in the United States. He was invited to join in on a game he was watching at a neighborhood playground. Patrick told the others he had never played before, but they still wanted him to participate. "They said it didn't make a difference," he later told filmmaker Spike Lee. "They just needed an extra body. So I played, I started, I messed up. . . . But I liked it, so I kept on playing, kept on getting better."[49]

The Education of a Ballplayer

Like many youngsters who had come to the United States from a different culture, Patrick experienced some problems in school. He had difficulty reading, and his thick Jamaican accent added to his problems by making it hard for his teachers to understand him. His mother, a firm believer in the importance of a good education, got him tutors and enrolled him in the Achievement School, a remedial center for junior high students in Cambridge. It was there that he played his first game of organized basketball.

Patrick was six feet, one inch tall when he entered the school, but within a year he

A young Patrick Ewing prepares for a free throw shot for his Rindge and Latin High School team.

had grown five inches. Like many other tall youngsters, he was very awkward. His willingness to work hard, however, began to pay off. By the time he entered Rindge and Latin High School in Cambridge, he had begun to show promise of becoming a very good player.

At Rindge and Latin, Patrick came under the tutelage of Mike Jarvis, the school's basketball coach. Jarvis indoctrinated him into the team-first style of the great Boston Celtics teams, which stressed players performing in particular roles for the good of the team. Patrick learned his lesson well. He was a hard worker, Jarvis told *New York Newsday*, "and if he didn't know something, he'd ask you a thousand times until he got it right. He became a star . . . but he wasn't always a great player. He went through times where he was clumsy and awkward. We had to tell him to be tall, walk tall, be proud of it."[50]

Patrick took a lot of kidding about his height during his first year on the varsity team. Describing his first game, he recalled, "People laughed at me that night too. All those people there, I was nervous. I scored one point and fouled out. They were saying I was clumsy. Yelling it out."[51]

By the time Patrick was a junior, he was even taller. He had shot up to six feet, eleven inches in height (he would reach seven feet as a senior) and was the star of the team, leading Rindge and Latin to two consecutive Massachusetts state championships. Patrick gained a measure of fame after his junior year when he was invited to try out for the 1980 U.S. Olympic team. Although he did not make the squad, he became the first high-school player ever to be invited to the tryouts.

In Patrick's senior year, he led his school to a third straight championship. Colleges all across the country were recruiting him, making him the most sought-after senior in the nation. To relieve some of the pressures involved in the recruiting process, Coach Jarvis sent out what became known as the Ewing Letter to approximately 150 colleges. In it, he spelled out Patrick's educational requirements. He explained that since Ewing had been living in the United States for only 6 years, he was struggling academically and might well need tutoring, remedial instruction, or tapes of lectures. Jarvis assured the schools that Patrick was a hard worker and would succeed both athletically and academically.

Nearly eighty schools responded to Jarvis's letter. Of those, sixteen were invited to make a presentation to Patrick and his parents. They eventually narrowed the list down to six schools. Patrick finally decided on Georgetown, where former Boston Celtic John Thompson was the basketball coach. As Ewing explained, "At any of the schools I visited, I would have gotten a great education, but I felt that Coach Thompson—he's seven feet, or six feet ten, and he played the center position—knows the position, and he was better equipped to teach me."[52] Patrick entered Georgetown as a freshman in the fall of 1981.

National Champions

In Ewing's very first year at Georgetown, he led the Hoyas to the championship game of the NCAA tournament. There, Georgetown was stopped by the University of North Carolina, 63–62, with a last-minute shot by another freshman by the name of Michael Jordan.

Ewing averaged 12.7 points and 7.5 rebounds per game for the Hoyas while playing excellent defense. Rumors began to circulate that he might leave school early to enter the NBA, but his mother put an end to such speculation. She insisted that he remain in school and graduate before turning professional.

In Patrick's junior year, he again led Georgetown to the championship game of the NCAA tournament. This time, however, the Hoyas were victorious. They defeated the University of Houston and its star center, Hakeem Olajuwon, by a score of 84–75. Ewing added to his list of impressive credentials by being named the Outstanding Player of the tournament. "It's frightening," said the University of Dayton's high scorer, Roosevelt Chapman. "Ewing is very mammoth. He's like an octopus with hands all over the place."[53]

Later that year, Ewing was named to the 1984 U.S. Olympic basketball team. He helped the squad win the gold medal in Los Angeles before returning to Georgetown for his senior season. There, he led the Hoyas to their third NCAA championship game in four years. They were the favorites to win a second consecutive national title, but their dreams were derailed by a gritty Villanova University team that came up with one of the greatest upsets in college basketball history in defeating Georgetown, 66–64.

Ewing celebrates with his Georgetown University teammates. Ewing earned many honors and awards during his college days, including a spot on the 1984 Olympic basketball team.

Despite the loss, Ewing won most Player of the Year awards and made the All-America team. The "Hoya Destroya," as he had become known, finished his college career as Georgetown's all-time leader in rebounds and blocked shots. Although his mother had died in 1983, Patrick fulfilled her wishes by graduating with a bachelor's degree in fine arts in June 1985. "Getting that degree," he told *Ebony* magazine, "meant more to me than an NCAA title, being named All-America, or winning an Olympic gold medal. I promised my mother before she died that I would graduate on time, and I'm proud to have fulfilled that promise."[54]

The Luck of the Draw

In his 4 years at Georgetown, Ewing forged a reputation as one of the greatest defensive players in college basketball history. He would unquestionably be the first player selected in the NBA draft that summer, but the team that would get that pick was still undecided. The league had just instituted a new lottery system that would determine the first seven choices in the draft. (Previously, the two last-place teams had flipped a coin to see who would pick first.) The names of the seven teams that failed to qualify for the playoffs the previous season were put in envelopes that were opened on May 12 by basketball commissioner David Stern. In a random drawing, the New York Knickerbockers won the first pick. With it, they selected Ewing on June 18. Three months later, he signed the largest contract ever by an NBA rookie, one that would assure him of $30 million over the next 10 years.

Ewing made his regular-season debut with the Knicks on October 26, 1985, against the Philadelphia 76ers at Madison Square Garden. Despite spraining his left ankle, he finished with 18 points and 6 rebounds in the New York loss. (The injury was an omen of things to come for Ewing, who would be plagued by an assortment of injuries throughout most of his pro career.)

Although the Knicks did not live up to the expectations of their fans (they would finish the season in last place, in large part because of injuries to key players Bernard King and Bill Cartwright), Ewing

Ewing accepts a hat from Knicks general manager DeBusschere after being chosen as the NBA's number one draft pick in 1985.

provided them with hope for the future with several exceptional performances. One occurred on Christmas Day against the Boston Celtics. Ewing helped bring New York back from a 25-point third-quarter deficit, scoring 18 points himself in the last quarter. The Knicks eventually won the game in double overtime. As Knicks coach Hubie Brown told Harvey Araton of the *New York Daily News* after the game, "Today [Ewing] surfaced as a real dominant force in the NBA."[55]

Michael Jordan challenges Ewing for the ball. Despite Ewing's contribution to the Knicks' appearance in the 1989 Eastern Division semifinals, the team was defeated by the Chicago Bulls.

Ewing led all first-year players in scoring average (20.0) and rebounding average (9.0). He missed 32 games because of injuries but was still named the league's Rookie of the Year. He was also named to his first All-Star Game, though he did not play because of an injury.

Turning the Corner

With center Cartwright recovered from his injury, Brown moved Ewing to forward the next season to allow the team to play the two big men at the same time. This strategy did not work, and, after getting off to a 4–12 start, Brown was fired. Ewing returned to center under new coach Bob Hill, and his play quickly improved. He finished the year averaging 21.5 points and 8.8 rebounds per game, but New York again finished in last place.

The Knicks did not get back on the winning track until Rick Pitino replaced Hill before the 1987–88 season. Employing the former Providence College coach's fast-break offense and full-court-pressing defense, the Knicks improved by 14 games to compile a 38–44 record. The next year, they improved by another 14 games to 52–30 and finished in first place in the Atlantic Division.

Ewing thrived under Pitino, as the two men had respect for each other. "I don't know if it was like college," recalled Ewing fondly, "but we did have fun . . . especially when we started to win. [Pitino] is a very rah-rah person, and we needed that, especially after the way my first two seasons were."[56] Ewing became one of the leaders of the team. He helped the club reach the Eastern Division semifinals in 1988–89, where they were stopped by the Chicago Bulls.

The special relationship between Ewing and his coach came to an abrupt end in 1989. That summer, Pitino resigned to return to the college ranks, where he accepted a job as head coach at the University of Kentucky. He was replaced on the Knicks' bench by Stu Jackson.

The Knicks' Main Man

Despite the coaching change, Ewing flourished in 1989–90. He finished third in the league in scoring, averaging a career-high 28.6 points per game. Included was a high of 51 points in a

March game against the Celtics. His total of 2,347 points broke a
New York team record that had stood since 1961–62. Ewing also
broke double figures in rebounds for the first time in his pro career, with an average of just under 11 per contest. He was even
more impressive in the playoffs, where he averaged 29.4 points
in New York's 10 games. Included were games of 44 points in the
first-round series against Boston and 45 in the division semifinals against the Indiana Pacers. For his excellent play, Ewing
was named to the All-NBA first team.

Ewing enjoyed another outstanding season in 1990–91, but
both he and the team struggled in the playoffs. Late that year, his
relationship with the Knicks' management became strained. According to the ten-year contract he had signed in 1985, Ewing had
the right to become a free agent in June 1991 if he was not one of
the four highest-paid players in the league. The team said he
ranked number four, but his agent disagreed. The matter eventually went before an arbitrator, who ruled in the team's favor.

Believing Ewing to be dissatisfied in New York, the Knicks
tried to trade him during the off-season but were unsuccessful. In
the meantime, New York had hired former Lakers coach Pat Riley to take over the club. Seeing this as a sign of the team's com-
mitment to winning, Ewing agreed to a new multiyear contract.

Disappointment in the Riley Years

In nine years as coach of the Lakers, Riley had won nine Pacific
Division titles. He quickly worked his magic to continue his
streak of first-place finishes with New York. Ewing again was superb in 1991–92. He ranked in the top ten in the league in scoring,
rebounding, and blocked shots. The Knicks' hopes for a title were
crushed by the Michael Jordan–led Bulls, who defeated New
York in a hard-fought seven-game conference semifinal series.

The loss would be one of several frustrating playoff defeats
suffered by Riley's Knicks. In 1992–93, the team lost to the Bulls
in the Eastern Conference finals after taking the first 2 games of
the series. The next year, Jordan announced his retirement and
the Knicks became one of the favorites to succeed the Bulls as
NBA champions. Unfortunately, the team came up just short of a
crown, losing to the Houston Rockets in a seven-game NBA finals series.

Riley's streak of first-place finishes ended with a drop to second place in 1994– 95. After eliminating the Cleveland Cavaliers in the first round of the playoffs, the Knicks were defeated by the Pacers in a classic seven-game Eastern Conference semifinals matchup. In the first game, the Pacers came from behind to deal New York a crushing loss as Reggie Miller scored 8 points in the final 16 seconds to wipe out a 5-point Knicks lead. New York won the second game, but the Pacers took the next two contests to move to within one game of advancing to the next round. With 5.9 seconds remaining in Game 5, Indiana's Byron Scott hit a 3-point shot to give the Pacers a 1-point lead. After the Knicks called a timeout, Ewing got the ball near the top of the key. He spun around and made a basket to give New York the win. Two days later, his 25 points and 15 rebounds led the Knicks to a 92–82 win to even the series at 3 games apiece.

The final game proved to be one of Ewing's most heartbreaking. With just seconds to go and the Pacers up by 2 points, he missed a driving layup that would have tied the contest. The Pacers moved on to the conference finals while Ewing and the Knicks went home, once again, without a championship. The loss was especially devastating to Pat Riley. The day after the finals ended, he stepped down as the team's head coach.

The End of the Line

The 1996–97 season was another one of disappointment for Ewing. With Larry Johnson and Allen Houston now members of the team, the Knicks won 57 games and finished second in the Atlantic Division. After sweeping the Charlotte Hornets in three games in the first round of the playoffs, the team faced the Miami Heat—now coached by Riley—in the division semifinals.

With New York leading the series, 3 games to 1, a fight broke out toward the end of Game 5. Although not involved in the brawl, Ewing and four other Knicks left the bench. The five players were suspended for one game since their action violated a league rule. With Ewing forced to sit out Game 6, the momentum shifted to Miami's favor. The Heat took 3 straight games from the depleted Knicks to move on to the division finals.

At age 36, Ewing made one last trip to the NBA finals in 1998–99. By that point, injuries had begun to take their toll on the Knicks captain. He appeared in just 38 games in the lockout-shortened season, helping the Knicks gain the eighth—and final—playoff spot in the Eastern Conference.

Along with newcomers Latrell Sprewell and Marcus Camby, the injury-saddled Ewing led the Knicks on an unforgettable run

Ewing posts up on Philadelphia 76er Matt Geiger during a 1999 game. Although Ewing's career was plagued by injuries, he was still a major presence on the basketball court.

past the Heat, Hawks, and Pacers. His season ended in the Indiana series, however, when he was sidelined by a partially torn tendon. Without their seven-foot center, the Knicks stood no chance against the San Antonio Spurs, who boasted a combination of their own in Tim Duncan and David Robinson. The Knicks lost in 5 games in what would be Ewing's last shot at an NBA title.

Good Bye, New York

Ewing played one more year with New York, but he was just a shell of his former self. Looking to rebuild, the Knicks sent him to the Seattle SuperSonics as part of a 4-team trade shortly before the start of the 2000–01 season. After one year with the Sonics, Ewing became a free agent. He signed with Orlando and played a backup role with the Magic in 2001–02. On September 17, 2002, he announced his retirement as an active player.

Ewing's pro career encompassed seventeen seasons in which he established himself as one of the dominant centers of his day. His deadly jump shot helped him post 24,815 points in the regular season and another 2,813 in the playoffs. He was also one of the foremost defensive centers in the history of the league. In addition to standing as the New York Knicks' all-time leader in nearly every major category, he was also an eleven-time NBA All-Star. Ewing never won an NBA championship but did win an NCAA title with Georgetown and two Olympic gold medals (1984, 1992).

At the same time Ewing announced his retirement, he also confirmed that he was joining the Washington Wizards as an assistant coach. In the hearts and minds of most fans, however, he will always be remembered as arguably the greatest New York Knick of all time.

CHAPTER 7

Latrell Sprewell

Not having played high-school ball until his senior year, Latrell Sprewell was a late bloomer by basketball standards. Still, he was selected by the Golden State Warriors in the first round of the 1992 draft. His road toward NBA stardom was sidetracked by an unfortunate 1997 incident in which he physically attacked Golden State head coach P. J. Carlesimo. After serving a suspension for his actions, Sprewell was traded to the Knicks. He has worked hard to repair his reputation and to regain his status as one of the league's top small forwards.

An Unsettled Childhood

Latrell Fontaine Sprewell was born to Latoska Fields and Pamela Sprewell on September 8, 1970, in Milwaukee, Wisconsin. Shortly after he was born, his parents moved the family—which included two daughters—to Flint, Michigan. Latrell rarely speaks of those early years. "I'm not into having people talking all about what I was like as a kid," he has said, "or what I did way back when. That's one of the things I always knew I wouldn't like about being in the public eye. I never asked to be famous."[57] One thing that is known about his home life is that he was close to his family. The people he says he admires most are his parents and grandparents.

Like many kids, Latrell enjoyed sports. He loved the Dallas Cowboys of the National Football League and dreamed of someday playing wide receiver for them. It was not until his senior year in high school, however, that he competed for any organized team.

By that time, Latrell's parents had separated. His mother moved back to Milwaukee, where she struggled to support the family by getting a job working in a factory. His father remained in Flint, where he made money by selling marijuana. Latrell lived there with his father for a while because his mother's boyfriend sometimes beat him. He enjoyed staying with his father because he did not have to worry about having enough food to eat or clothes to wear. As he said, "Just having stuff was different at that point."[58]

Latrell Sprewell remains a hard-working and talented basketball player despite the controversies surrounding his personal life.

When Latrell was 16 years old, his father's illegal activities finally got him into trouble. Latoska Fields was arrested on charges of possession of drugs with intent to distribute. When he was sent to jail, Latrell returned to live with his mother in Milwaukee. "That was hard," recalled Latrell. "I only visited him in jail once. After that, I was back with my mother. I didn't see him much."[59]

In Milwaukee, Latrell attended Washington High School. One day, while walking through the halls at the beginning of his senior year, he was approached by James Gordon, the school's basketball coach. Gordon invited him to try out for the team, which he did. "He was six-four already, 170 and strong," recalled Gordon. "I knew an athlete. Latrell had big, rawboned hands, and his biceps were all knots—knots upon knots."[60]

One of Sprewell's most impressive qualities was his willingness to work to improve his game. As Gordon said, "What made him good was his work ethic. If you suggested he work on free throws instead of dunking, he'd go straight to the free throw line."[61] Not only did he make the squad, he immediately became the team's star. He averaged 28 points per game in his only season, made All-City, and led Washington to the city conference final.

Making a Name for Himself

Because of his limited playing experience, Latrell was not recruited by any Division I colleges after graduating from high school. He eventually enrolled at Three Rivers Community College in Poplar Bluff, Missouri. In his freshman year of 1988–89, he averaged 16.5 points per game in 26 contests. (He was suspended for several games when he and a couple of teammates were arrested for shoplifting batteries from a convenience store.)

The next year, Latrell increased his average to 26.6 points while pulling down 9.1 rebounds per game. He set a school single-season scoring record while leading Three Rivers to a 32–8 record. In addition to his ability to put the ball in the basket, his hard work helped him earn a reputation as a standout player on defense.

After playing 2 years at the junior-college level, Sprewell began to draw the interest of several Division I schools. One of these was the University of Alabama, located in Tuscaloosa. He eventually accepted a scholarship to the school and spent his first summer making up course work and working on improving his game. After classes, he spent every day alone in the gym, shooting 300 three-point shots. According to Sprewell, it was "the summer I learned how to shoot the ball."[62]

Sprewell's teammates at Alabama included future NBA performers Robert Horry, Jason Caffey, and James Robinson. Playing alongside other talented players, Sprewell shone. He averaged just 8.9 points per game in 1990–91 but further enhanced his reputation as a standout defender. In his senior year, he doubled his average to 17.8 points and led the team in scoring. He also averaged 5.2 rebounds, 2.1 assists, and 1.8 steals per game. Sprewell led the Southeastern Conference in minutes played with 36.2 per game and was named to the All-Southeastern Conference team. He led coach Winfrey "Wimp" Sanderson's Crimson Tide to a 26–9 record and a spot in the postseason NCAA tournament. Sanderson remembered Sprewell as a player who never caused problems. "I had no emotional situations with him, for good or for bad," he recalled. "He played to win games."[63]

An Exciting Start

After graduating from Alabama in 1992 with a degree in social work, Sprewell was selected by the Golden State Warriors as the 24th overall pick in the first round of the NBA draft on June 24, 1992. His selection was greeted by boos from many of the Warrior fans in attendance who knew little about him and wanted the Warriors to draft a better-known player.

Playing guard for coach Don Nelson's squad, the six-foot, five-inch, 195-pound Sprewell soon won the fans over. He put together a solid freshman season, averaging 15.4 points, 3.8 assists, 3.5 rebounds, and 1.6 steals per game. He led Golden State in minutes played and became the first rookie in club history to record 1,000 points, 250 rebounds, 250 assists, 100 steals, and 50 blocks in a single season. Sprewell earned a spot on the NBA All-Rookie second team, leading all newcomers in assists and three-point shooting.

As impressive as his first season was, Sprewell truly burst into prominence in his sophomore year. With several of Golden State's key players sidelined by injuries, Nelson looked to him to pick up the slack. He responded in magnificent fashion. At the age of 23, Sprewell led the Warriors in scoring, averaging 21 points per game. He did this while playing more minutes than anyone else in the entire league (3,533). "The guy is just tireless," raved Nelson. "The amazing thing isn't just that he plays so many minutes, it's that he's got as much energy in the 40th minute as he does in the first."[64] For his all-around excellence, Sprewell was named to the All-NBA first team and the NBA

All-Defensive second team. He was also selected to play in his first All-Star Game, registering 9 points and 7 rebounds in the midseason contest.

Turbulent Times

The 1994–95 season was one of controversy for Sprewell. It began when his teammates—and close friends—Chris Webber and

Sprewell excited Golden State Warriors fans with dramatic play like this slam dunk. During his rookie year there he broke several team records.

Billy Owens were traded to other teams. Sprewell was upset by the deals and responded by writing their uniform numbers on the backs of his shoes in protest. With Webber and Owens gone, he began to receive more attention in the media as the team's star. A private person by nature, Sprewell began turning down interviews, which did not endear him to the press. "I don't think people need to know that much about my private life," he had said earlier that year. "I just want to be judged on what I do on the court."[65]

As a result of personality clashes Sprewell also began to feud with Nelson and several of his teammates, particularly Tim Hardaway (whom he considered Nelson's pet) and Jerome Kersey. His problems with Kersey erupted when the two began scuffling one day during practice. After leaving the court, Sprewell returned with a two-by-four board. The altercation was finally ended when he was pulled away by teammates.

Sprewell was suspended twice during the season for conduct detrimental to the team. He received even more negative publicity when his four-year-old daughter Page suffered several bites on her face and had her ear severed after being attacked by one of his four pit bulls. When questioned about the attack by *San Francisco Chronicle* reporter Tim Keown, Sprewell seemed strangely unconcerned. "That stuff happens," he reportedly said. "People die every day. Maybe if it had been more serious, it would have affected me."[66]

Despite his problems with Nelson, his teammates, and the media, Sprewell suffered just a slight dropoff in his performance on the court. He again led the Warriors in scoring (20.6 points per game) and was named as a starter for the West squad in the 1995 All-Star Game.

The following year, Sprewell seemed more content. Nelson resigned when the team got off to a slow start and Hardaway was traded to the Miami Heat. Sprewell became the team's captain and franchise player and responded with another all-star performance. He led Golden State in scoring for the third straight year (18.9 points per game) and in steals (1.63 per game). The Warriors rewarded him with a new four-year $32 million contract that made him one of the highest-paid guards in the league.

Coach P.J. Carlesimo and Sprewell were often at odds, and tension between the two men ran high.

Sprewell followed up with another solid season in 1996–97. He averaged a career-high 24.2 points per game (fifth in the league) and added 19 more as a starter in the All-Star Game. Unfortunately, the Warriors did not show any significant improvement in the standings. With the team stumbling, the front office named P. J. Carlesimo head coach in June 1997. The move would change Sprewell's life forever.

The Incident

Carlesimo had a reputation for being loud and profane and extremely hard on his players. It did not take long for Carlesimo and Sprewell to clash. In early November, the Warriors were losing to the powerful Los Angeles Lakers. During a time-out, Carlesimo saw his star laughing in the huddle. He told the team to get serious, and when Sprewell failed to do so, his coach sent him to the bench. In front of the rest of the team, Sprewell reportedly said, "You're a (expletive) joke."[67] The incident resulted in Carlesimo keeping him out of the starting lineup for the Warriors' next game.

Shortly afterward, Sprewell was thrown out of a practice and fined for missing a team plane. With the team doing poorly, he said he wanted to be traded. Since the tension between the coach and his star was at such a high pitch, the Warriors came close to dealing Sprewell to the San Antonio Spurs.

On December 1, the Warriors were running through a drill during practice. Unhappy with the club's performance, Carlesimo told Sprewell to "put a little mustard on those passes." Sprewell, convinced that he was being made the scapegoat for the club's poor performance, told Carlesimo, "I don't want to hear it today."[68]

The confrontation escalated with the two men in each other's faces. Finally, Sprewell reportedly said, "I'll kill you,"[69] and began choking Carlesimo. (Sprewell later offered a slightly different version of what happened. "I wasn't choking P.J.," he said. "P.J. could breathe. It's not like he was losing air or anything like that. . . . It wasn't a choke. I wasn't trying to kill P.J."[70])

Teammates separated the two men and Sprewell left the arena. He returned about 10 minutes later and again confronted Carlesimo. Witnesses said Sprewell punched his coach, but he denied doing so. As it turned out, the fact that he came back to the gym affected the harshness of the penalty Sprewell received since it seemed to indicate that the action was premeditated. As NBA commissioner David Stern said, "It wasn't so much the choking that got Latrell such a severe punishment. It was coming back after he'd had time to cool off."[71]

Repercussions

Although he later issued an apology to his family and fans (but not to Carlesimo), Sprewell was almost universally condemned for his actions. The Warriors reacted by immediately suspending him, then terminating his contract (which had $25 million remaining) two days later. He was suspended by the NBA for one year and became a symbol of all that was wrong with modern professional athletes. "This is a clear matter of right and wrong," said Warriors general manager Garry St. Jean. "There is no issue to compromise. Outrageous conduct by players in pro sports has been tolerated for too long. We are drawing the line."[72]

Some observers, however, were sympathetic to Sprewell. It was suggested that Carlesimo's comments were racially motivated and that the player was justified in striking back. Several players came forth to back Sprewell's assertion that he had been provoked. Others supported him by confirming that Carlesimo's behavior was often abusive and confrontational.

At a press conference, Latrell Sprewell apologizes for choking Carlesimo.
Many players and fans were sympathetic to Sprewell, noting that Carlesimo's
behavior was often abusive.

The NBA Players' Association filed a grievance against the league and the matter eventually went to arbitration. Arbitrator John Feerick ruled that the punishment was excessive. The NBA suspension was reduced by six months and the Warriors were ordered to reinstate Sprewell's contract.

The Road Back

It was obvious that Sprewell had worn out his welcome with Golden State. By this time, however, NBA players and owners were engaged in a bitter labor dispute. Nothing could be done until a new agreement was reached in January 1999.

Soon afterward, the Warriors traded him to the New York Knicks in exchange for John Starks, Chris Mills, and Terry Cummings.

Like several other teams, the Knicks were eager to give Sprewell a second chance. "Latrell is one of the top talents in the game on both the offensive and defensive ends," said New York Knicks president Ernie Grunfeld. "When you get the opportunity to improve your club with a three-time All-Star such as Latrell, you have to pursue it. We expect him to become an integral part of our team."[73]

Sprewell seemed intent on repairing his damaged reputation. At a press conference after his official reinstatement, Sprewell again apologized. "I'm sorry," he said. "We all make mistakes. I made one. I said I'm sorry about that, and I'm asking for a second chance. I'm not someone who has an attitude problem. I'm not mean. People may think that because of the aggressive way I play the game, but I don't walk around the streets like that."[74]

Sprewell's mistake cost him 68 games of the 1997–98 season and approximately $6.4 million in salary. The Knicks hoped he would bounce back to become an important part of their offense. He started off on the right foot by pouring in 24 points and grabbing 6 rebounds in his very first game against the Orlando Magic, on February 5.

The Knicks struggled through the shortened season but managed to earn the final playoff spot in the Eastern Conference. Sprewell made his presence felt despite missing 13 games because of a stress fracture in his right heel. He averaged 16.4 points (second on the team to Patrick Ewing) and 4.2 rebounds per game coming off the bench in a sixth-man role (the first substitute off the bench).

The Knicks surprised everyone in the playoffs, defeating the Miami Heat, Atlanta Hawks, and Indiana Pacers to advance to the NBA finals, where they eventually lost to the Spurs. With Ewing hampered by injuries, Sprewell played more minutes in the postseason. He finished as the team's leading scorer, averaging 20.4 points per game. Sprewell's outstanding play helped New York advance further in the playoffs than any other eighth-seeded club had ever gone.

A New York Favorite

Sprewell won over the New York fans with his hard-nosed play
and willingness to put the team's interests ahead of individual
statistics. Knicks coach Jeff Van Gundy was not surprised. "It's
all about evolving," he told the *New York Times*. "When you're
part of an environment that places a standard on winning, your
thinking changes. When you talk to Latrell now, he never talks

*Sprewell drives to the basket in a 1999 finals game against the San Antonio
Spurs. Sprewell became a New York favorite with his aggressive play and
unselfish teamwork.*

about points or shots. All he talks about is team. He is completely unselfish."[75]

Sprewell continued to turn his image around in 1999–2000. He started every game and averaged 18.6 points per contest. During the season, he scored the 10,000th point of his career, picked off his 2,000th rebound, garnered his 2,000th assist, and saw his 20,000th minute of action.

These personal achievements, however, were secondary compared with his major goal of winning a championship. Unfortunately, he would not reach that goal in 2000. Despite his best efforts, the Knicks lost to the Pacers in the Eastern Division finals to come up short in their quest.

Sprewell continued to put up good numbers in 2000–01 and 2001–02, finishing second on the team in scoring to Alan Houston in both seasons. Salary cap problems, however, plagued the Knicks in their attempt to put together a championship team. The club hit a low point in 2002 when it failed to qualify for the playoffs for the first time since 1987.

Although the Knicks have struggled on the court, Sprewell's drive to excel helped make him one of the team leaders. In addition, he continued to make great strides toward improving his image. The change in the public's perception of him was dramatic. NBA commissioner Stern even gave him permission to appear in television ads promoting the league. Such a thing would have been unthinkable five years before.

Off the court, Sprewell spends time with his family and tinkers with his cars. The reluctant star still guards his privacy, preferring to let his play speak for him. He has gradually grown into the role of the team's unofficial spokesman and seems much more at ease with the media. He has worked hard to show people that the events of December 1, 1997, were an aberration. As he told Chris Broussard of the *New York Times*, "The image now, hopefully, is a positive one."[76]

More Problems

Unfortunately, that image took another hit prior to the start of the 2002–03 season. When the Knicks' players arrived for media day on September 30, Sprewell showed up with a broken hand. He said the injury happened when he fell aboard his yacht, but the *New York Post* reported he injured it when he got into a fight on the boat. A week later, the Knicks fined him $250,000 for not informing them of the injury. They also told him to stay away from team practices until he was able to contribute. Sprewell responded by saying he would fight the fine.

Tensions between the team and its star player continued to escalate. Sprewell announced he was suing the *Post* for the story that said he had injured the hand in a fight. At the same time, he criticized management for various decisions they had made. Later that same day, the Knicks said Sprewell had been suspended for an exhibition game for not sticking to his rehabilitation assignment. The suspension meant he would not be paid 1/90th of his salary, or approximately $137,500.

Sprewell's situation threw a shadow over the preseason. Although no official announcement was made, it seemed likely the Knicks would try to trade him as soon as he was able to show he had recovered from the broken hand. The unfortunate situation was fast becoming a media circus. Whether Sprewell can overcome this latest public relations uproar remains to be seen.

What is certain is that the team that engages his services will get a player who brings energy and excitement to the game and a will to win that is second to none. His ability to score and play defense has helped make him an All-Star in the past. His desire to be part of a championship team is the goal that continues to push him to excel.

New York Knicks Achievements

Year-by-Year Records

Season	Coach	Finish	Wins	Losses	Playoff Wins	Losses
1946–47	Neil Cohalan	3rd/Eastern Div.	33	27	2	3
1947–48	Joe Lapchick	2nd/Eastern Div.	26	22	1	2
1948–49	Joe Lapchick	2nd/Eastern Div	32	28	3	3
1949–50	Joe Lapchick	2nd/Eastern Div.	40	28	3	2
1950–51	Joe Lapchick	3rd/Eastern Div.	36	30	8	6
1951–52	Joe Lapchick	3rd/Eastern Div.	37	29	8	6
1952–53	Joe Lapchick	1st/Eastern Div	47	23	6	5
1953–54	Joe Lapchick	1st/Eastern Div.	44	28	0	4
1954–55	Joe Lapchick	2nd/Eastern Div.	38	34	1	2
1955–56	Joe Lapchick 26–25 Vince Boryla 9–12	T3rd/Eastern Div.	35	37	—	—
1956–57	Vince Boryla	4th/Eastern Div.	36	36	—	—
1957–58	Vince Boryla	4th/Eastern Div.	35	37	—	—
1958–59	Andrew Levane	2nd/Eastern Div.	40	32	0	2
1959–60	Andrew Levane 8–19 Carl Braun 19–29	4th/Eastern Div.	27	48	—	—
1960–61	Carl Braun	4th/Eastern Div.	21	58	—	—
1961–62	Eddie Donovan	4th/Eastern Div.	29	51	—	—
1962–63	Eddie Donovan	4th/Eastern Div.	21	59	—	—
1963–64	Eddie Donovan	4th/Eastern Div.	22	58	—	—
1964–65	Eddie Donovan 12–26 Harry Gallatin 19–23	4th/Eastern Div.	31	49	—	—
1965–66	Harry Gallatin 6–15 Dick McGuire 24–35	4th/Eastern Div.	30	50	—	—
1966–67	Dick McGuire	4th/Eastern Div.	36	45	1	3

Season	Coach	Finish	Wins	Losses	Playoff Wins	Losses
1967–68	Dick McGuire 15–22 Red Holzman 28-17	3rd/Eastern Div.	43	39	2	4
1968–69	Red Holzman	3rd/Eastern Div.	54	28	6	4
1969–70	Red Holzman	1st/Eastern Div.	60	22	12	7
1970–71	Red Holzman	1st/Atlantic Div.	52	30	7	5
1971–72	Red Holzman	2nd/Atlantic Div.	48	34	9	7
1972–73	Red Holzman	2nd/Atlantic Div.	57	25	12	5
1973–74	Red Holzman	2nd/Atlantic Div.	49	33	5	7
1974–75	Red Holzman	3rd/Altantic Div.	40	42	1	2
1975–76	Red Holzman	4th/Atlantic Div.	38	44	—	—
1976–77	Red Holzman	3rd/Atlantic Div.	40	42	—	—
1977–78	Willis Reed	2nd/Atlantic Div.	43	39	2	4
1978–79	Willis Reed 6–8 Red Holzman 25–43	4th/Atlantic Div.	31	51	—	—
1979–80	Red Holzman	T3rd/Atlantic Div.	39	43	—	—
1980–81	Red Holzman	3rd/Atlantic Div.	50	32	0	2
1981–82	Red Holzman	5th/Atlantic Div.	33	49	—	—
1982–83	Hubie Brown	4th/Atlantic Div.	44	38	2	4
1983–84	Hubie Brown	3rd/Atlantic Div.	47	35	6	6
1984–85	Hubie Brown	5th/Atlantic Div.	24	58	—	—
1985–86	Hubie Brown	5th/Atlantic Div.	23	59	—	—
1986–87	Hubie Brown 4–12 Bob Hill 20–46	T4th/Atlantic Div.	24	58	—	—
1987–88	Rick Pitino	T2nd/Atlantic Div.	38	44	1	3
1988–89	Rick Pitino	1st/Atlantic Div.	52	30	5	4
1989–90	Stu Jackson	3rd/Atlantic Div.	45	37	4	6
1990–91	Stu Jackson 7–8 John MacLeod 32–35	3rd/Atlantic Div.	39	43	0	3
1991–92	Pat Riley	T1st/Atlantic Div.	51	31	6	6
1992–93	Pat Riley	1st/Atlantic Div.	60	22	9	6
1993–94	Pat Riley	1st/Atlantic Div.	57	25	14	11
1994–95	Pat Riley	2nd/Atlantic Div.	55	27	6	5
1995–96	Don Nelson 34–25 Jeff Van Gundy 13–10	2nd/Atlantic Div.	47	35	4	4
1996–97	Jeff Van Gundy	T2nd/Atlantic Div.	57	25	6	4

Season	Coach	Finish	Wins	Losses	Playoff Wins	Losses
1997–98	Jeff Van Gundy	2nd/Atlantic Div.	43	39	4	6
1998–99	Jeff Van Gundy	4th/Atlantic Div.	27	23	12	8
1999–00	Jeff Van Gundy	2nd/Atlantic Div.	50	32	9	7
2000–01	Jeff Van Gundy	3rd/Atlantic Div.	43	34	2	3
2001–02	Jeff Van Gundy 10–9					
	Don Chaney 20–43	7th/Atlantic Div.	30	52	—	—
Totals			2229	2109	179	171

NBA Most Valuable Player
(Maurice Podoloff Trophy)
Selected by vote of NBA players until 1979–80; by writers and broadcasters since 1980–81.

1969–70	Willis Reed, New York

IBM NBA Coach of the Year
(Red Auerbach Trophy)
Selected by writers and broadcasters.

1969–70	Red Holzman, New York
1992–93	Pat Riley, New York

Schick NBA Rookie of the Year
(Eddie Gottlieb Trophy)
Selected by writers and broadcasters.

1964–65	Willis Reed, New York
1985–86	Patrick Ewing, New York
1987–88	Mark Jackson, New York

J. Walter Kennedy Citizenship Award
Selected by the Pro Basketball Writers Association.

1980–81	Mike Glenn, New York
1985–86	Rory Sparrow, New York

NBA Sixth Man Award
Selected by writers and broadcasters.

1994–95	Anthony Mason, New York
1996–97	John Starks, New York

NBA Finals Most Valuable Player
Selected by writers and broadcasters.

1970	Willis Reed, New York
1973	Willis Reed, New York

Statistical Leaders
(Based on average per game.)
Scoring

Season	Points	
1984–85	32.9	Bernard King, New York

Field-Goal Percentage

Season	Points	
1958–59	.490	Ken Sears, New York
1959–60	.477	Ken Sears, New York

Three-Point Field-Goal Percentage

Season	Points	
1981–82	.439	Campy Russell, New York

Steals

Season	No.	
1979–80	3.23	Micheal Ray Richardson, New York

(Based on season total.)
Minutes

Season	No.	
1995–96	3,457	Anthony Mason, New York

Rebounding

Season	No.	
1953–54	1,098	Harry Gallatin, New York

Assists

Season	No.	
1949–50	396	Dick McGuire, New York
1979–80	10.1 per game	Micheal Ray Richardson, New York

Personal Fouls

Season	No.	
1974–75	330	Phil Jackson, New York
1976–77	363	Lonnie Shelton, New York
1977–78	350	Lonnie Shelton, New York
1987–88	332	Patrick Ewing, New York

Disqualifications

Season	No.	
1984–85	16	Ken Bannister, New York

Notes

Chapter 1: An NBA Institution

1. Quoted in George Kalinsky, *The New York Knicks: The Official 50th Anniversary Celebration*. New York: Macmillan, 1996, p. 5.
2. Quoted in Kalinsky, *The New York Knicks*, p. 11.
3. Quoted in Mitch Lawrence, "Big Deals," *New York Daily News*, November 1, 1996, Special Section, p. 8.

Chapter 2: Willis Reed

4. Quoted in Larry Fox, *Willis Reed*. New York: Grosset & Dunlap, 1973, p.7.
5. Quoted in Charles Moritz, ed., *Current Biography Yearbook: 1973*. New York: H.W. Wilson, 1973, p. 348.
6. Quoted in Fox, *Willis Reed*, p. 16.
7. Quoted in Fox, *Willis Reed*, p. 43.
8. Quoted in Fox, *Willis Reed*, p. 46.
9. Quoted in Fox, *Willis Reed*, p. 52.
10. Quoted in Fox, *Willis Reed*, p. 75.
11. Quoted in Fox, *Willis Reed*, p. 87.
12. Quoted in Fox, *Willis Reed*, pp. 104–105.
13. Quoted in Thom Loverro, "Mountains of Men," *Sport*, February 1989, p. 61.

Chapter 3: Walt Frazier

14. Walt Frazier and Joe Jares, *Clyde: The Walt Frazier Story*. New York: Grosset & Dunlap, 1970, p. 18.
15. Quoted in Moritz, ed., *Current Biography Yearbook: 1973*, p. 141.
16. Frazier and Jares, *Clyde*, p. 45.
17. Quoted in Frazier and Jares, *Clyde*, p. 241.
18. Quoted in Frazier and Jares, *Clyde*, p. 66.
19. Quoted in Frazier and Jares, *Clyde*, p. 240.
20. Quoted in Frazier and Jares, *Clyde*, p. 171.

21. Quoted in "Walt Frazier," *Knicks 4 Life*. www.knicks4life.com.

22. Quoted in "Walt Frazier," *Knicks 4 Life*.

23. Quoted in "Walt Frazier," *Greater Talent Network, Inc.* www. greatertalent.com.

24. Quoted in Josh Elliott, "Walt Frazier, Debonair Knick," *Sports Illustrated*, April 16, 2001, p. 16.

Chapter 4: Bill Bradley

25. Quoted in Charles Moritz, ed., *Current Biography Yearbook: 1965*. New York: H.W. Wilson, 1965, p. 50.

26. Quoted in Moritz, ed., *Current Biography Yearbook: 1965*, p. 50.

27. Quoted in Invensys. www.invensys.com.

28. Bill Bradley, *Life on the Run*. New York: Quadrangle, 1976, p. 34.

29. Quoted in Moritz, ed., *Current Biography Yearbook: 1965*, p. 50.

30. Quoted in Moritz, ed., *Current Biography Yearbook: 1965*, p. 51.

31. Quoted in Charles Moritz, ed., *Current Biography Yearbook: 1982*. New York: H.W. Wilson, 1982, p. 45.

32. Quoted in Moritz, ed., *Current Biography Yearbook: 1965*, p. 51.

33. Quoted in Moritz, ed., *Current Biography Yearbook: 1965*, p. 51.

34. Bradley, *Life on the Run*, p. 35.

35. Bradley, *Life on the Run*, p. 36.

36. Quoted in Kalinsky, *The New York Knicks*, p. 52.

37. Quoted in Red Holzman with Leonard Lewin, *My Unforgettable Season—1970*. New York: Tor Books, 1993, p. 50.

38. Quoted in Barton Gellman and Dale Russakoff, "At Princeton, Bradley Met Impossible Demands," *Washington Post*, December 13, 1999.

39. Bradley, *Life on the Run*, pp. 210–11.

40. Holzman with Lewin, *My Unforgettable Season—1970*, p. 91.

41. Quoted in Jonathan Roos, "Bradley's Life Shows a Man Driven to Win at Everything," *Des Moines Register*, November 28, 1999.

Chapter 5: Red Holzman

42. Red Holzman and Harvey Frommer, *Red on Red*. New York: Bantam Books, 1987, p. 8.

43. Quoted in Holzman and Frommer, *Red on Red*, p. 15.
44. Quoted in Holzman and Frommer, *Red on Red*, p. 29.
45. Quoted in Holzman and Frommer, *Red on Red*, p. 41.
46. Holzman and Frommer, *Red on Red*, p. 56.
47. Quoted in Holzman and Frommer, *Red on Red*, p. 60.
48. Quoted in Holzman and Frommer, *Red on Red*, p. 184.

Chapter 6: Patrick Ewing

49. Quoted in Charles Moritz, ed., *Current Biography Yearbook: 1991*. New York: H.W. Wilson, 1991, p. 203.
50. Quoted in Moritz, ed., *Current Biography Yearbook: 1991*, p. 203.
51. Quoted in Kalinsky, *The New York Knicks*, p. 164.
52. Quoted in Moritz, ed., *Current Biography Yearbook: 1991*, p. 203.
53. Quoted in Jim Savage, *The Encyclopedia of the NCAA Basketball Tournament*. New York: Dell, 1990, p. 532.
54. Quoted in Moritz, ed., *Current Biography Yearbook: 1991*, p. 204.
55. Quoted in Moritz, ed., *Current Biography Yearbook: 1991*, p. 205.
56. Quoted in Moritz, ed., *Current Biography Yearbook: 1991*, p. 205.

Chapter 7: Latrell Sprewell

57. Quoted in Phil Taylor, "Center of the Storm," *Sports Illustrated*, December 15, 1997, p. 62.
58. Quoted in Eric Konigsberg, "The Real Spree," *New York Magazine*, April 19, 1999.
59. Quoted in Konigsberg, "The Real Spree."
60. Quoted in Konigsberg, "The Real Spree."
61. Quoted in Taylor, "Center of the Storm," p. 67.
62. Quoted in Konigsberg, "The Real Spree."
63. Quoted in Konigsberg, "The Real Spree."
64. Quoted in Phil Taylor, "Latrell Sprewell," *Sports Illustrated*, February 21, 1994, p. 75.
65. Quoted in Taylor, "Center of the Storm," p. 67.
66. Quoted in Taylor, "Center of the Storm," p. 67.
67. Quoted in Taylor, "Center of the Storm," p. 62.
68. Quoted in Taylor, "Center of the Storm," p. 62.
69. Quoted in Konigsberg, "The Real Spree."

70. Quoted in Roger Simon, "Latrell Sprewell's Genius," *Jewish World Review*, March 13, 1998. www.jewishworldreview.com.
71. Quoted in Konigsberg, "The Real Spree."
72. Quoted in *Newsweek*, "Sprewell Rebounds into the Game," March 16, 1998.
73. Quoted in Clifford Thompson, ed., *Current Biography Yearbook: 2001*. New York: H.W. Wilson, 2001, p. 518.
74. Quoted in Phil Taylor, "A Real Stretch," *Sports Illustrated*, February 1, 1999, p. 53.
75. Quoted in Thompson, ed., *Current Biography Yearbook: 2001*, p. 518.
76. Quoted in Thompson, ed., *Current Biography Yearbook: 2001*, p. 519.

For Further Reading

Books

Peter C. Bjarkman, *The Biographical History of Basketball*. Chicago: Masters Press, 2000. A fascinating look at the history of basketball through the biographies of more than 500 of the game's most famous and significant personalities.

Zander Hollander and Alex Sachare, eds., *The Official NBA Basketball Encyclopedia*. New York: Villard Books, 1989. This volume contains complete statistical records for every player to appear in an NBA game.

Red Holzman and Harvey Frommer, *Holzman on Hoops*. Dallas: Taylor, 1991. Recollections of a life in basketball by the former head coach of the New York Knicks.

John McPhee, *A Sense of Where You Are*. New York: Noonday Press, 1978. An intimate portrait of Bill Bradley as a college student and athlete.

Bob Spitz, *Shoot Out the Lights*. New York: Harcourt Brace, 1995. An entertaining look at the New York Knicks' first championship season.

Mike Wise and Frank Isola, *Just Ballin'*. New York: Simon & Schuster, 1999. The story of the chaotic rise and fall of the 1999 New York Knicks.

Works Consulted

Books

Bill Bradley, *Life on the Run*. New York: Quadrangle, 1976. Bradley's own account of the life of a professional athlete.

Larry Fox, *Willis Reed*. New York: Grosset & Dunlap, 1973. The inspirational story of Knicks captain Willis Reed.

Walt Frazier and Joe Jares, *Clyde: The Walt Frazier Story*. New York: Grosset & Dunlap, 1970. Walt Frazier's own story, from his childhood in Atlanta through the Knicks' 1969–70 championship season.

Red Holzman and Harvey Frommer, *Red on Red*. New York: Bantam Books, 1987. The autobiography of the architect of the New York Knicks championship teams of the 1970s.

Red Holzman with Leonard Lewin, *My Unforgettable Season—1970*. New York: Tor Books, 1993. Coach Red Holzman's personal memoir of the Knicks' championship season of 1969–70.

George Kalinsky, *The New York Knicks: The Official 50th Anniversary Celebration*. New York: Macmillan, 1996. A photographic history of the Knicks through the eyes of Madison Square Garden photographer George Kalinsky.

Charles Moritz, ed., *Current Biography Yearbook: 1965*. New York: H.W. Wilson, 1965. Library volume that contains all of the biographies published in *Current Biography* magazine in 1965.

———*Current Biography Yearbook: 1973*. New York: H.W. Wilson, 1973. Library volume that contains all of the biographies published in *Current Biography* magazine in 1973.

———*Current Biography Yearbook: 1982*. New York: H.W. Wilson, 1982. Library volume that contains all of the biographies published in *Current Biography* magazine in 1982.

————*Current Biography Yearbook: 1991.* New York: H.W. Wilson, 1991. Library volume that contains all of the biographies published in *Current Biography* magazine in 1991.

Jim Savage, *The Encyclopedia of the NCAA Basketball Tournament.* New York: Dell, 1990. The history of the first fifty-two years of the NCAA Basketball Tournament.

Clifford Thompson, ed., *Current Biography Yearbook: 2001.* New York: H.W. Wilson, 2001. Library volume that contains all of the biographies published in *Current Biography* magazine in 2001.

Periodicals

Josh Elliott, "Walt Frazier, Debonair Knick," *Sports Illustrated,* April 16, 2001.

Barton Gellman and Dale Russakoff, "At Princeton, Bradley Met Impossible Demands," *Washington Post,* December 13, 1999.

Eric Konigsberg, "The Real Spree," *New York Magazine,* April 19, 1999.

Mitch Lawrence, "Big Deals," *New York Daily News,* November 1, 1996.

Thom Loverro, "Mountains of Men," *Sport,* February 1989.

Newsweek, "Sprewell Rebounds into the Game," March 16, 1998.

Jonathan Roos, "Bradley's Life Shows a Man Driven to Win at Everything," *Des Moines Register,* November 28, 1999.

Phil Taylor, "Center of the Storm," *Sports Illustrated,* December 15, 1997.

————"Latrell Sprewell," *Sports Illustrated,* February 21, 1994.

————"A Real Stretch," *Sports Illustrated,* February 1, 1999.

Internet Sources

Roger Simon, "Latrell Sprewell's Genius," *Jewish World Review,* March 13, 1998. www.jewishworldreview.com.

"Walt Frazier," *Greater Talent Network, Inc.* www.greatertalent.
com.

"Walt Frazier," *Knicks 4 Life*. www.knicks4life.com.

Website

Invensys (www.invensys.com) The official website of Invensys,
a global leader in the management of production and energy
resources. The site includes a biography of Bill Bradley, who
was a speaker at an Invensys symposium.

Index

Picture Credits

About the Author

John F. Grabowski is a native of Brooklyn, New York. He holds a bachelor's degree in psychology from City College of New York and a master's degree in educational psychology from Teacher's College, Columbia University. He has been a teacher for thirty-three years, as well as a freelance writer, specializing in the fields of sports, education, and comedy. His body of published work includes forty-one books; a nationally syndicated sports column; consultation on several math textbooks; articles for newspapers, magazines, and the programs of professional sports teams; and comedy material sold to Jay Leno, Joan Rivers, Yakov Smirnoff, and numerous other comics. He and his wife, Patricia, live in Staten Island with their daughter, Elizabeth.